Other books by Carter and Minirth

The Anger Workbook

The Freedom from Depression Workbook

The Choosing to Forgive Workbook

The Worry Workbook

The Anger Trap

People Pleasers

Just Like Us

The Anger Workbook
for Christian Parents

The Anger Workbook
for Christian Parents

Dr. Les Carter and Dr. Frank Minirth

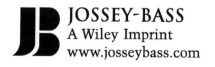
JOSSEY-BASS
A Wiley Imprint
www.josseybass.com

Published by Jossey-Bass
A Wiley Imprint
One Montgomery Street, Suite 1200, San Francisco, CA 94104-4594   www.josseybass.com

Scripture taken from the NEW AMERICAN STANDARD BIBLE®, Copyright © 1960, 1962, 1963, 1968, 1971, 1972, 1973, 1975, 1977, 1995 by The Lockman Foundation. Used by permission.

All cases cited in this book are composites of the authors' actual cases in their practices at Minirth-Meier Clinic. Names and specific details have been changed to maintain confidentiality.

Jossey-Bass books and products are available through most bookstores. To contact Jossey-Bass directly call our Customer Care Department within the U.S. at 800-956-7739, outside the U.S. at 317-572-3986, or fax 317-572-4002.

Jossey-Bass also publishes its books in a variety of electronic formats. Some content that appears in print may not be available in electronic books.

ISBN: 978-0-787-96903-5

FIRST EDITION

PB Printing   10 9 8 7 6 5 4 3 2

CONTENTS

PREFACE and ACKNOWLEDGMENTS

If you have a teen or a preteen in your home, it is certain that anger will surface. The decade prior to the entrance into adulthood holds many exciting challenges and learning opportunities for our youth, and that creates the potential for bonding experiences as well as conflict between parents and their young. Youths are predictably eager to find their independence and set out on their own path toward maturity, but we adults naturally want them to exercise wisdom and restraint in this quest. Therein lies the potential for conflict.

Do you and your young ones have a well-defined game plan for managing the anger that accompanies this conflict? Most families do not. In fact, despite the fact that family members love one another and want the best for one another, they readily find themselves embroiled in strain that can threaten the stability of the family unit. It is this potential that we want to help you avert.

Throughout the book, we write from a distinctly Christian perspective. Although we believe that Christian doctrine clearly addresses the matter of our eternal destiny, we hold to the notion that the ethics of Christianity can be useful in all arenas, particularly the home. As therapists who speak daily with individuals about a healthy way of life, we freely discuss how to incorporate Christian principles into everyday circumstances. We particularly want to impress upon our clientele that our manner of living is the element that carries the most clout as we attempt to teach our youth eternal truths. Perhaps our philosophy could be summarized by the notion that who you are is the best way to illustrate what you truly believe. With that thought in mind, we hope to inspire parents to live in a loving manner so the beautiful message of God's love can be incorporated by our children naturally. Even in the presence of anger in the home, we can determine to be a conduit for God's love if we learn to understand how anger can be managed in ways that uphold dignity and respect.

In *The Anger Workbook for Christian Parents,* we begin with the premise that if our youths are ever going to learn proper ways of handling anger, their interests are best served when their parents establish the appropriate model first. Parents need to recognize why anger exists and what an angry person is trying to accomplish. They need to know what choices, both good and bad, are available to the angry person, and how to apply the good choices. Then they need to confront the inner issues (control, insecurity, fear) that feed conflict to be best suited to handle anger with respect and purpose.

As parents make inroads in managing their anger appropriately, they are then positioned to teach their youths to join them in the good effort. As anger is reasonably contained, parents are then positioned to be guides who can credibly talk with their kids about their relationship with God, and how their spiritual life can be a vibrant and relevant part of everyday life. It is not our purpose to discuss in this book how to evangelize your children, but it is our purpose to help you keep anger from defining your family atmosphere, so that your efforts to spiritually influence your children can remain on the appropriate track.

What do you think? Are you up to the task? Reflect on your own youth and the conflict you surely experienced with your own parents. How often did they take the time to discuss rationally with you the reasons for your anger and how you could manage it well? If you are like most, you would admit that this did not happen. Would you have benefited if anger had been a clearly understood emotion? Of course!

This workbook is intended to be used by parents who want to give their kids every advantage in the process of finding relationship and emotional maturity. We have provided tools to help you personalize the information given. Checklists help you specify the many facets of anger management. "What about you?" questions are asked for the purpose of having you relate the book's contents to your home. At the end of each chapter is a guide for family discussion, presented for the purpose of allowing the entire family to gather together to understand each other more fully and to plan together how to keep unruly anger from overtaking the home. As a parent you can benefit from reading each chapter and responding to the questions, but you may find it beneficial to sit down with your kids once a week and go over each chapter's information and then engage in the guided questions at the chapter's end.

Also, we have learned that our past workbooks are used extensively in group and classroom settings. With that in mind, we have included at the end of each chapter questions that can be used in such settings. Our aim is to stimulate open sharing and the exchange of ideas that can prove helpful in generating hope and encouragement among parents seeking the same goals.

You will notice that we refer to case illustrations to further clarify the concepts discussed in each chapter. Please be aware that for confidentiality reasons we have carefully altered the identity of the people "on display." Nonetheless, their stories and experiences are quite true. We hope their efforts will inspire you to make similar inroads in creating a home atmosphere that balances the use of anger.

We have been most appreciative of those who assisted us in the preparation of this book, including Vickie Gage, Brian Wade, and especially Meagan Nichols. Also, between the two of us, we have seven girls, without whom we could not have written with any personal insights. They are Cara, Megan, Rachel, Renee, Carrie, Allie, and Liz.

Richardson, Texas   Dr. Les Carter
January 2004   Dr. Frank Minirth

TWELVE STEPS TOWARD
ANGER MANAGEMENT FOR PARENTS

Step 1: Learn to identify what is behind the expression of anger, and make that a primary focus.

Step 2: Be aware of the ways you may choose to handle anger poorly, so you can be specific in your efforts to improve.

Step 3: When you have a responsible message to communicate, do so in a way that upholds the dignity of the others involved.

Step 4: Have a strong sense of purpose as a parent in order to respond to anger-producing circumstances as an initiator, not a reactor.

Step 5: Realize that the best way to be in control is to diminish control tactics, speaking instead about choices.

Step 6: Refuse to lord over your child, but speak instead as one who believes in the equal worth of each family member.

Step 7: Let humility be your guide as you demonstrate to your children that selfishness has no place in successful anger management.

Step 8: Don't be threatened by an adversarial response, but be confident in your own response.

Step 9: Respect the fact that each family member is responsible for his or her choices.

Step 10: Identify the false assumptions that feed your anger, and let truth guide your decisions in discipline.

Step 11: Identify your own outside stressors that create anger, and choose to address them separately, as opposed to bringing them into parental communication.

Step 12: Set aside an attitude of defeat, and recognize that in each situation you can choose to be an overcomer.

The Anger Workbook
for Christian Parents

1

THE PURPOSE OF ANGER

STEP 1: Learn to identify what is behind the expression of anger, and make that a primary focus.

It was the best of times. It was the worst of times." These are the opening words of Charles Dickens's *A Tale of Two Cities*. Certainly Mr. Dickens did not intend to apply them to the life of teenagers and preteens. His focus was quite separate. Hardly any parent, however, would refute these words as an apt description of life in a home with maturing youths.

As children begin to take on the looks and thoughts of adults-in-waiting, they can be a delight, given their ability to relate with a keener mind and increased wit and higher reasoning. Parents can actually enjoy a young person's enhanced abilities to contribute to the overall good of the household more fully than in previous years. It can be a blessing that the child has greater capacity for maintaining responsibilities and communicating with deeper awareness. The youth's increased desire for independence, when channeled appropriately, is the beginning of interactions with parents that are less authoritarian and more typical of the mutual respect that exists in a healthy adult relationship.

That same desire for independence, however, can be the impetus for great friction in the home. In most parent-teen relationships, a built-in friction exists because young people's overconfidence in themselves invariably clashes with their parents' desire for caution. Eager to spread their wings for flight, our youths may deem the wisdom of their elders unnecessary, only to discover that the elders are none too eager to be so summarily dismissed. The net result is ongoing conflict played out in the form of arguing, bargaining, and manipulation. The emotion beneath this conflict is anger.

Do you have a well-conceived plan for handling that anger? Do you know how to respond wisely when your young refute you? Have you taken the time to discern your own reasons for feeling angry? Do you recognize how patterns of control, insecurity, or fear can sabotage the emotional well-being of the home?

As you take the time to pore over the information in the pages to follow, you will be challenged to understand the anger that is sure to exist between yourself and the youths in your home. We are writing with the belief that the best way to teach your youngsters to handle anger appropriately is first to be aware of your own use of anger. Only as you understand your own emotional responses and how best to proceed with them can you guide your young in their emotions.

Most Christians are familiar with the traits listed in Galatians 5:22–23 as the fruit of the Spirit: love, joy, peace, patience, kindness, goodness, faithfulness, gentleness, and self-control. These certainly represent the qualities most desired by the majority of parents as they address conflict with their young. How often, though, do these traits go flying out the window as sons and daughters act defiantly or disobediently? Anger has a way of running roughshod over parents' best-laid plans; before they know what hit them it takes priority over the fruit of the Spirit, and the home atmosphere is ruined.

Our goal, as we work with parents, is to help them understand the nature of anger and learn how to tame it so anger allows them to teach their young the ways of God. If anger remains a constant in parent-and-child interaction, the young person's emotional and spiritual development is hindered greatly. On the other hand, if anger is managed in a balanced manner, the groundwork is laid for deeper teaching about the paths of the righteous.

Let's begin with a fundamental realization. Some parents will say, "I don't feel angry very often, but I do have regular experiences with frustration and irritability." In saying this, they show a misunderstanding of anger. Implied in such a comment is the notion that anger is displayed only through loud, raucous behavior such as shouting or slamming doors. If you do not engage in such behavior, so the reasoning goes, you are not experiencing anger.

Indeed, anger is often accompanied by noisy and forceful communication, but it is not that narrow in scope. Frustration *is* anger. Irritability is anger. Likewise, anger is in play when you feel impatient, when you cling to critical thoughts, when you are annoyed, and when you punish through withdrawal. Anger is a broad emotion; it can be experienced whether you are loud or silent.

No doubt, you have heard that you should never discipline your children in anger. This represents a noble thought, but it does not run parallel with reality. Being a parent, you *are* going to have many moments of agitation, disgust, or annoyance. In other words, you will feel angry toward your children just as they will feel angry toward you. Not only are these reactions not strange, but they commonly become the motivation that spurs you to address problems. Rather than trying to have (or pretending you have) no feelings of anger, it is best to admit its presence so you can then make informed decisions about the wisest way to proceed.

Ephesians 6:4 instructs fathers not to provoke their children to wrath. This is not meant to be a biblical injunction against having anger in the home, but to handle anger-producing conflicts in a manner that is healing rather than harmful. Instead of determining never to have anger, it is more realistic to first learn to identify the many ways in which anger can be expressed, for the purpose of then choosing to address the anger in the most constructive way. Trying to be anger-free as a parent is not a realistic goal. Trying to recognize the reasons for the anger so as to be most effective in family communication *is* a realistic goal.

Ephesians 4:26 tells us to "be angry, and yet do not sin," meaning that it can be normal to have angry emotions. Just a few verses prior to that, in Ephesians 4:15, we find the phrase "speaking the truth in love," which implies that directness and confrontation can still be managed within a respectful framework. Whenever anger exists in your home (which it inevitably does), you have the option to manage it cleanly or to handle it in a less-than-constructive way. Our goal is to teach clean uses of anger that diminish the probability of ongoing dispute.

An Illustration

Rita spoke with Dr. Carter about her struggles with her two sons, Ryan and Ashton. They were twelve and fifteen, respectively. "Those boys are the two most competitive people on the planet," she explained. "Their communication with each other is an ongoing battle for an edge over the other. Naturally, since Ashton is older he usually has the upper hand in their arguments, but Ryan is pretty feisty, and he thinks he can outwit his brother on just about anything."

Their family life had many of the same tensions as any other. The boys argued over which television shows they wanted to watch. Among the four family members there was one computer, and of course the boys would argue about who was spending more time using it. Sometimes the computer was needed for homework assignments, other times it was desired for pleasure. Arguments that began over a minor subject, perhaps using the computer, would often gain an irrational momentum and turn into a nasty fight that included shouting and insulting words, and worse. Ryan and Ashton frequently appealed to their mother to pronounce judgment upon the other's lack of fair play.

For her part, Rita would try to play referee as calmly as possible, but on days when the bickering seemed both absurd and endless, she could explode. "What is it about you two that makes you feel you can spend your entire day arguing?" Her voice would be tense and condescending. Of course, such questions only fanned the flames, and never did she find good results by shouting and accusing. Nonetheless, friction and open conflict regularly visited their home as the same old broken patterns of communication were employed.

How about you? In what circumstances do you find yourself getting pulled in by your kids' behavior? (For instance, "My son will tell me exactly what he knows I want to hear, and then he'll do whatever he wants to do," or "If I'm going to get my daughter to do anything, I've got to constantly push her to get it done.")

_____

_____

_____

Proverbs 29:22 reminds us that "an angry man stirs up strife and a hot tempered man abounds in aggression." How does your misuse of anger stir up strife in your kids once they see your anger on display? (For instance, "My son won't say a word, but I know he's thinking defiant thoughts," or "My daughter may break down in tears and protest that I just don't understand.")

_____

_____

_____

Recognizing that Rita was flustered because she seemed too easily prone toward anger, Dr. Carter wanted to ease her harsh self-assessment: "You're not wrong or out of place to be feeling what you feel. Virtually any parent is going to dislike having to monitor two sons who seem to bicker constantly. If anything, you take the first step toward taming your anger when you admit that you feel it. It's hard to make healthy adjustments without first being keenly aware of its presence."

To help you begin learning how to handle anger wisely as a parent, let's first get a good idea of some of the many ways it can be shown. Look over this list and determine which responses are common in you and which are common in your children. You might place the appropriate initials beside the behaviors that fit with each family member.

_____ Impatience over matters of presumed urgency
_____ Open griping and complaining
_____ Sulking and withdrawal
_____ Offering rebuttals while not really showing understanding

_____ Doing the opposite of what is expected ("I'll show you")

_____ Easy or regular criticizing

_____ Verbal expressions of annoyance and displeasure

_____ Speaking in an adversarial tone of voice

_____ Being persuasive or coercive

_____ Name calling or character assassination

_____ Having to be right, even when it promotes friction

_____ Displays of an "I don't care" attitude

_____ Use of sarcasm

_____ Unwillingness to hear a differing perspective

_____ Inability to accept those who have erred

_____ Chronic stubbornness

_____ A habit of quitting

_____ Holding onto a grudge

_____ Speaking ill of people behind their back

_____ Pushing ideas or preferences in an overbearing manner

It's quite a list! Which of these forms of anger are most common in yourself?

_____

_____

_____

Which of these forms of anger would your children say are most common in you?

_____

_____

_____

Which of these forms of anger are most common in your children?

_____

_____

_____

Rita commented to Dr. Carter: "It's interesting to see how each of us in our family handles anger differently. Each of us has moments when we speak sharply or we get pulled into an adversarial style. I've noticed, though, that Ashton tends to try to keep a strong upper hand both against his little brother and against me. He can be the stubbornest person in the house as he'll just tune the rest of us out and do whatever he wants, knowing full well that he's creating friction. I actually think he enjoys it."

"How does this influence the rest of you?" asked Dr. Carter.

"Well, Ryan can't be quiet. He'll pitch a flying fit when his brother belittles him, and he's very capable of pestering his brother and me until he gets his way. If things don't unfold as he likes, then he goes into a meltdown and he'll sulk.

"Me, I'm all over the place with my anger," Rita continued. "Sometimes I'll shout at the boys, sometimes I'll ignore them and tell them to work it out without me. Sometimes I get hooked lecturing them, but that only turns into a loud debate. I wish my husband would take more of a lead in addressing these situations, but he's a conflict-avoider. He'll withdraw, and some days we won't hear from him for hours at a time."

Wanting to teach some positive skills, Dr. Carter said, "It's easy to conclude that methods of handling anger in your home leave much to be desired. Let's look beyond the ineffective methods of communication, though, and see if we can find anything right or good about the anger."

"Good?" came Rita's reaction. "You're suggesting there is something good in all this?"

"That's what I'm suggesting," replied the doctor. "Let's go down to the very core of your anger and determine what you're really trying to accomplish. If you could focus on the bottom-line message that is pushing your anger, it would help you determine how to communicate it more effectively."

The Purpose of Anger

Sure enough, anger can seem like an ugly, troublesome emotion having no place in a home that is trying to achieve peace or cooperation. Parents are often so focused on the poor behavior that accompanies anger that they miss the legitimate message spurring it in the first place. Let's not overlook the fact, though, that you might have something *right* to say in your anger. Likewise, though your children may not behave in a desirable way, amid all their anger there may be a legitimate message that needs to get out.

Think for a moment about what you are trying to accomplish each time you have anger to express. Undoubtedly, at the instant you feel angry, you are sensing that there is something not right in your environment. You are feeling ignored, dismissed, criticized, misunderstood, or rejected. Your anger, then, is acting as a push toward self-preservation. You want to be taken seriously. You want to feel that your voice is heard. Your anger could be understood as a motivation to do something to correct the things that are wrong.

Ephesians 4:26 indicates that there are certainly times when your anger can be an appropriate response ("Be angry, but without sin"). When your anger is triggered by one of your children, what is the valid message you want to communicate at that very moment? (For instance, "When my daughter whines time and again about time limits for the phone, I want her to respect my decisions and to recognize that I'm being reasonable," or "Whenever my son ignores me, I want him to show me some respect.")

_____

_____

_____

Can you recognize that your anger is spurred by a good goal? Though your methods may not always be the best, there is legitimacy in your message.

Now shift gears. You may not like the way your son or daughter expresses anger or acts defiantly, yet are you willing to acknowledge that the child may also have something legitimate pushing his or her anger? For instance, Ashton would express anger toward his younger brother, Ryan, because he did not respect his desire to use the computer. As their arguments over such matters escalated into ugly exchanges, it would become evident that disrespect was flying back and forth between the two boys. Their discussion would quickly deteriorate into ugly accusations, and then finally Ashton would speak in agitation to his mother about the situation. Even if Ashton was less than pleasant in presenting his arguments, he still might have an understandable concern. (So might Ryan, for that matter.)

Think of some common incidents when your children express anger. Even if they do a poor job communicating it, what might be reasonable about what they feel? (For instance, "My son complains that he doesn't get to do as much with his friends as he would like. I realize that peer acceptance is very important to him and he's indicating that he wants to feel accepted," or "When my daughter balks at having to do homework, it's understandable that she might be feeling burned out with so many assignments.")

_____

_____

_____

Sometimes anger can be pushed along by sheer selfishness or insensitivity (more on that in later chapters), but there is often a message at the base of each person's anger that deserves to be heard. Be willing to stand firmly in your own legitimate anger, and be willing to search out the reasonable message behind the child's anger.

Anger Defined

Ultimately, anger is the emotion of self-preservation. Whether it is handled cleanly or insensitively, the angry person is motivated to preserve one of three things: personal worth, perceived needs, or basic convictions. Let's break these down one by one to get a more thorough understanding of anger's purpose.

Preserving Personal Worth

As Rita interacted with her two sons, she often entertained the thought, *These boys are showing me very little respect, and I'm tired of it!* Not only was it reasonable to desire respect from them, it was also reasonable for her to teach them to honor her and one another in their communication. In fact, it would be irresponsible for her *not* to address the issue of her personal worth when her boys showed disrespect.

Dr. Carter explained to Rita, "Don't apologize for wanting to stand up for your worth. A central truth in the Christian message is that each person has God-given value. We are each at our most effective state when we recognize the fact that we are highly prized by God. If each of us feels capable of standing upon that value and if we recognize it in others, our communications will be rewarding. Your home is a laboratory where you and your sons are conducting experiments in human relations. They will take those experiments into the world, so it's good for them to learn that respect and worth need to be acknowledged."

In your home, how is your anger linked to your drive to preserve personal worth and respect? (For instance, "I want my kids to realize that people in leadership and authority deserve to be given proper consideration," or "They can learn that the best way to be treated in a worthy manner is to treat others that way first.")

_____

_____

_____

Let's turn the tables. Your children may not be sophisticated yet in managing their frustrations, but they too seek respect when feeling anger. How is their anger a cry to be treated as a person of worth? (For instance, "When my daughter gripes about our limits regarding her way of dressing, she's indicating that she wants us to see her as one who deserves trust," or "My son thinks I'm invalidating his worth when I veto his decision to go out with friends I don't think are good for him.")

_____

_____

_____

It is quite easy to focus on the immaturity or irresponsibility of your kids' reasoning. Parents easily make the mistake of getting drawn into arguments about kids' poor choices in behavior or priorities, ignoring their hunger to be upheld as worthy. This only increases the anger because the young person feels invalidated. To defuse the building anger, it is helpful to focus on the need beneath the anger rather than the poor behavior that accompanies it.

Rita had a potential problem on her hands one day when Ryan was especially insistent that he should be allowed to see a movie she did not believe to be appropriate. "You always say no to everything," came his exaggerated complaint. "My friends' parents aren't nearly as strict on them. Why can't I do what they get to do . . . just once?"

Her normal reply might have been to argue the merits of the movie or to defend her style of parenting. But remembering the discussion about anger being linked to the drive for worth, she chose another route: "Ryan, I'm beginning to realize just how important it is for you to feel like you fit in with your friends. That makes sense to me. I'm still not in favor of the movie, but let's talk about how we can handle our priorities so you won't feel so left out."

Ryan was still annoyed at her decision, but his mother persisted in showing him that she would explore further options regarding peer involvement. It did not erase *all* of his anger at that moment, but she was establishing herself as one who would take his desire for acceptance seriously.

In the same manner, you too can respond differently to your child's anger by focusing less on the errant demand and more on the cry for respect that lies behind the anger. How might this transform your reaction to your child's anger? (For instance, "I'd argue less about how right I am, and I would focus more on why my daughter feels hurt," or "I'd see my son's anger as an opportunity to learn what's really going on deep inside.")

_____

_____

_____

Preserving Legitimate Needs

We humans are interdependent. As we attempt to build lives of satisfaction, our chances for success increase if we recognize each other's normal needs and work together in a spirit of cooperation. Certainly a family system presents many occasions where cooperation can greatly improve the quality of life for each member.

Whenever family members experience anger, there is a strong likelihood that the angry one is thinking, *You don't care at all about my needs, and I wish I could correct that problem.*

Consider some of the simple needs that exist in ordinary family interaction:

• The need for coordination in chores and domestic duties
• The need for encouragement and friendliness
• The need to protect and care for personal properties
• The need to respect schedules and time requirements
• The need for wisdom regarding money management
• The need for helpfulness during times of illness or duress
• The need to respect individual uniqueness or differentness
• The need for courtesy
• The need to maintain satisfactory ties with friends and extended family
• The need for spiritual growth and stimulation

As you think about your needs as a parent, which ones stand out most? (For instance, "I need my kids to recognize that they are not the only ones who use the phone," or "I need them to coordinate schedules with me.")

_____

_____

_____

Dr. Carter explained to Rita: "When you're angry with your sons, you're probably feeling at that moment that they show low regard for the needs that are part of your daily routine. The anger may be expressed as impatience or annoyance, but at the base of your emotion can be a perfectly normal desire."

"I've never really thought much about what I'm trying to accomplish with my anger," she admitted. "All I know is that when I'm ticked off, I just feel like I'm trying to light a fire under my boys, or I'm just playing referee." Then she reflected, "You know, now that you've pointed it out, I can see how my anger is tied to the fact that my needs are lacking."

When your needs are ignored by one of your kids, why do you so regularly respond with irritability or frustration? (For instance, "Forcefulness seems to be the only way I can get my son to cooperate," or "I'm constantly exasperated because no one in my home seems to realize that I have needs too.")

_____

_____

_____

_____

As you observe how your kids behave with little regard for your needs, it is easy to dismiss their anger as wrong. Are you willing to recognize that in their emotion they too are feeling their needs are not being addressed? Through the years, it is part of your task as a parent to help them distinguish true needs from selfish wants. Nonetheless, rather than focusing strictly on their poor behavior you can indicate that you recognize their perceived needs. This effort falls in line with the instruction given in James 1:19, which states that we do best when we are "quick to hear, slow to speak, and slow to anger." Listening for the purpose of deciphering your child's needs can go a long way toward defusing the tension that accompanies their emotion.

What needs do your kids seem to feel are not adequately addressed in your home? (For instance, "My daughter has a high need for social stimulation, so when I restrict access to her friends she feels that need is being slighted," or "My son thinks he needs the latest computer stuff, and he gets ticked off when he senses that I'm not cooperating with him.")

_____

_____

_____

Parents make a major mistake in trying to convince their young that their needs are not warranted. In many cases, the parents may actually be correct to recognize that kids can feel convinced their needs are of the utmost importance, when in fact they are not. It is common knowledge that selfish motives or a feeling of entitlement can drive young people as they communicate their preferences and desires. Knowing this, parents may feel it is their task to immediately correct the child's feelings, explaining how their demands are unreasonable. The result is almost always an ugly standoff between parent and child.

Dr. Carter spoke with Rita about how to address her sons' needs. "The first rule when you address your sons' anger is that you not invalidate their perceived needs, no matter how off-base they may seem to be. Before you address the matter at hand, you can help diffuse the anger by indicating that you're willing to consider the feelings they're expressing."

As an example, Ryan came to his mother agitated and complaining that Ashton was being rude as he (Ryan) was spending time with his (Ryan's) friends: "Why does he think he can just come along and take over whenever my friends are here to see me? I hate it when he's so selfish that he can't just leave us alone."

In the past, Rita would have scolded him for feeling hate, and she might have told him to quit complaining and get a better attitude. But this time, she used a more understanding approach: "Ryan, I hear that you need time to develop your friendships in your own manner without your brother's interference. That makes sense to me. Let's talk about how we can accomplish that with the least amount of arguing."

Before you correct your kids' errant displays of anger, choose to speak to the unmet need that is driving the emotion. Once that is accomplished, the probability increases that the rest of your message will be heard.

Preserving Basic Convictions

In addition to preserving worth and needs, anger is linked to preserving our most basic convictions. When you feel angry, there is almost always a core belief that has not been upheld. In expressing anger, you are indicating that you cannot sit idly as you observe others living contrary to what you know is right.

Consider some of the fundamental convictions that tend to arouse people's anger:

- Family members and friends should honor human decency.
- Lying has no place in a growing relationship.
- Punctuality and cleanliness are reflections of respect for others.
- Foul language taints constructive communication.
- It is wise and good to apologize and say "I was wrong."
- A critical spirit poisons a relationship. Encouragement is greatly preferred.
- One person cannot shoulder the entire load required to run a household. Teamwork is essential.
- It is rude to invalidate someone's feelings or perceptions.
- It is necessary to manage money wisely, as opposed to spending it frivolously.
- Time spent with extended family members must be balanced with the needs of the immediate family.

As you contemplate the convictions that spur you toward expression of anger, which stand out as most common? (For instance, "You have to consider how others feel before you make a decision affecting their lives," or "When a parent speaks, a child shouldn't be allowed to simply stare at the TV and ignore what is being said.")

_____

_____

_____

What is right about holding to your convictions? (For instance, "I believe that it's the parents' job to teach relationship skills to the kids," or "I want my son to grow up with a defined set of values.")

_____

_____

_____

It is vital for you to maintain good convictions, but it is also possible to go too far to the extent that stubbornness, rigidity, or condemnation results. Angry parents often have excellent beliefs to instill in their young ones, but the method can be so condescending or insulting that the legitimate message is lost. We Christians can be quite vulnerable to this problem because we *know* right from wrong and we feel that we are being disloyal to our values if we are seen as soft. For example, Rita recognized that she wanted to instill the value of a cooperative spirit in her two sons. As she admitted, though, "I feel a strong obligation to make sure my kids are brought up with the right principles. But sometimes I speak with such exasperation in my voice that their only thought is to get away from me. They don't hear what really needs to be heard."

How about you? How might you stand up for your convictions, but in a manner that sabotages the message? (For instance, "When I explain to my daughter how she needs to be orderly with her things in the house, I'm using such a sharp tone of voice that she feels unaccepted by me," or "I tell my son he needs to appreciate the value of a good day's work, but he gets the message that I just think he is lazy and has no redeeming value.")

Be willing to acknowledge that your children have convictions, too, when they feel angry. Although their use of anger may not be fully mature, are you willing to go behind the scenes and address the conviction? For example, Dr. Carter said to Rita: "On several occasions you've mentioned how Ryan becomes upset when his older brother taunts him or interferes with his friendships. Sure enough, I'm guessing that Ryan may sound whiny when he complains, but let's take the time to determine the convictions he's holding onto."

Rita thought for a moment and then stated: "I know that Ryan's big issue is fairness. He really is pretty conscientious about respecting separate property or priorities. Ashton, on the other hand, has the attitude that he can claim anything that belongs to his brother as if it's his, too. Ryan becomes flustered when his brother doesn't share the same conviction."

Even as Rita needed to guide Ryan in learning to communicate his anger more constructively, it was good to help her son see that he had beliefs worth listening to. She correctly reasoned that Ryan would be more open to her guidance once he recognized that she could acknowledge that he had a reasonable conviction that deserved attention.

When your children become angry, be willing to look beyond the poor method of communication so as to find the convictions that drive it. What convictions seem most commonly associated with your kids' anger? (For instance, "When my daughter gripes about having to do homework, she's holding to the belief that her teen years should consist of more than just boring assignments," or "When my son is angry at his girlfriend, it's because loyalty means more to him than it does to her.")

_____

_____

_____

Whether or not you agree wholly with your child's convictions, are you willing to openly acknowledge them for the purpose of having a constructive conversation? How do you suppose this can change the way anger is managed in your home? (For instance, "In our home, no one seems to feel understood, but I would change that by offering my understanding," or "Instead of rebutting with my opinions, I could slow down and let my daughter explain her opinions more fully.")

_____

_____

_____

The beginning point of managing anger fairly in your home is to recognize that it is often driven by something legitimate. Because most of us, though, tend to be too negative or insensitive when we communicate anger, it is easy to dismiss anger as invalid. Before doing so, ask yourself:

- What is reasonable about my anger, and how can I adjust my method of communication so that the viable message is more digestible?
- What is it that my child is communicating in his or her anger that I need to be more attentive to?
- Can we make room for the fact that anger exists in our home and agree to address it in a manner consistent with the deeper issue of Godly love?

In the next two chapters, we begin to explore the many options you have, both good and bad, for handling anger. Then we go deeper by examining the reasons we opt for poor choices over constructive choices.

For Family Discussion

1. Reexamine the many ways in which anger can be expressed, as listed earlier in this chapter. One by one, have each family member identify the top three or four ways they display anger. Then let each person give feedback to one another regarding how they can tell when the other family members are angry.

2. Let all the family members identify their own needs and convictions they wish the rest of the family would consistently respect.

3. Let each family member have a turn being the focus person. The rest of the family has the assignment of identifying what is probably legitimate about the focus person's experiences of anger.

4. Being as constructive as possible, go back to each family member one at a time and let the rest of the family take turns offering suggestions as to how each person can communicate legitimate anger more appropriately.

5. Once again, take turns focusing one at a time on each individual. Have each member of the group express to the focus person how he or she is willing to ease that person's anger by choosing to hear what is being said when anger is expressed.

For Further Reflection

Ephesians 4:26 states, "Be angry and yet do not sin; do not let the sun go down on your anger." Let's break this verse down for further thought.

1. Since the Bible states that we may be angry, there are times when this emotion has an appropriate purpose. When is your anger as a parent appropriate? What might be appropriate about the anger felt by your children?

2. Anger is to be managed without sin. What attitudes or behaviors might accompany your anger, turning it into a sinful response? How does the "sin nature" influence the way your children respond when they feel angry?

3. By not letting the sun go down on your anger, the Scripture presumes that anger can be managed in an immediate time frame; it does not have to linger. When does this instruction prove to be difficult in your home? What causes anger to linger overnight, perhaps for days or even weeks at a time? How do the family priorities need to change to keep anger from lingering too long?

James 1:19 states, "Let everyone be quick to hear, slow to speak, and slow to anger."

4. Being slow to anger does not mean that anger should be eliminated, but managed judiciously. How can you determine if you as a parent are being slow and judicious in handling your anger?

5. How is the anger of your children affected if you choose to be quicker to hear? What do they want you to know about their feelings?

Proverbs 29:22 reminds us: "An angry man stirs up strife, and a hot tempered man abounds in transgression."

6. When does anger cross the line and become destructive? Why do you allow your anger to become a strife-producing communication? Why are your children willing to engage in such an exchange of anger?

2

HOW ANGER IS MISMANAGED

STEP 2: Be aware of the ways you may choose to
handle anger poorly, so you can be specific
in your efforts to improve.

Although anger can have a valid purpose in family relationships, unfortunately, it is not often managed constructively. Repeatedly we
have heard parents say that they have good intentions when they address conflict, but something happens to worsen the circumstances. We
hear explanations like these:

"I usually begin with calm emotions, but once my son starts talking
back, that's more than I can handle, so I become livid."

"For my whole life, I've been exposed to yelling, and when I get
tense that's what I do."

"I get so flustered with my kids that I just shut down. I've been
known to go hours without saying a word."

"The only way I can get my daughter's attention is to be forceful.
That's the only language she'll listen to."

"My kid has a real smart mouth, and that really sets me off. I'll usually explain in no uncertain terms that I am *not* going to be treated
with ridicule."

Each of the sentiments that accompany your angry moments can be understandable. Your child may be disrespectful or uncooperative or belligerent, and certainly it is normal that you would feel angry. You may assume, though, that you have no alternative but to go with the flow of the moment, meaning your anger will be less than productive. Would you be willing to acknowledge, though, that your methods of handling anger are the result of choices? While you are in the heat of conflict, it may seem as though you are responding on pure instinct, yet your mind is actively engaged, telling you how to respond. When you respond poorly in anger it is because you have chosen to do so. Are you willing to examine your poor choices so you can be aware of how you defeat yourself? This is a step in the direction of making healthy adjustments.

Likewise, your children are making choices in how they communicate anger. Throughout childhood they need to develop an awareness regarding the many options they have in the management of their anger. In the preteen years, you can begin coaching them by discussing the fact that they have options, and by talking about what those options are. The deeper the children go into their teen years, you can talk about the meatier ingredients that push the anger along, toward desirable or undesirable conclusions. You can also talk with them about how your use of anger can reflect your commitment to be anchored in spiritual strength, letting traits such as respect and decency anchor your communications. Before you can be the guide they need, though, you have to examine your own choices regarding anger and be aware of how anger can easily get out of hand. Are you up to it?

Healthy anger expression is summarized in a succinct phrase tucked inside Ephesians 4:15: "Speaking the truth in love." People feeling angry want to impress others of truth related to personal dignity, needs, and convictions. In a world that is certain to produce conflict, it is necessary for family members to openly express concerns for the purpose of clearing the way for love. Unfortunately, most individuals do not think loving thoughts in the midst of their angry feelings, and therein lies the potential for great disaster as the emotions flow.

Dr. Minirth worked with a man, Bronson, who had a history of mismanaged anger. His anger outbursts were so common and so disruptive that they had decided to use a medical approach to help him. An SSRI antidepressant was prescribed, and sure enough his mood leveled out nicely. The doctor explained to Bronson, "Sometimes anger outbursts can be tempered when a medical approach is used, but we can't rely on medicine alone to help you through this problem. We'll need to give special attention to the choices you make when you feel angry so you can learn to give highest priority to the better way."

As Dr. Minirth got to know Bronson, he learned that his family was all over the board in how they would handle their anger. Bronson admitted, "When I was a boy, the only remembrance I have of anger was my dad's rages. He'd sound off at the most minor offenses, and there was no telling what he'd say or do. He'd curse or he might throw something or he'd give major spankings. I was always intimidated by him, and sometimes I honestly hated him." Then, shaking his head, he added, "I can't stand to admit it, but I've become my own father."

Bronson had three children, boys aged seventeen and fourteen and a daughter aged eight. "With my daughter I can be fairly patient because she's a pretty compliant child," he said. "But my sons bring out the worst in me. The older one, Jonathan, is a duplicate of me, and he can go off like a rocket when he gets ticked off, which is pretty often. My second son, Cody, learned a long time ago that he could never win an argument with either me or his older brother, so he holds a lot in and then gets into mischief behind my back."

"What about your wife?" came the doctor's question. "Where does she fit into the mix?"

"Well, Carol honestly doesn't know what to do with the rest of us. Lots of times she'll just cry when I get mad or when Jonathan unloads on one of the others. Sometimes she may get loud, but it never gets her anywhere good. Sometimes she just holds it all in. I think she has problems with depression, although I don't really like to talk with her about that sort of thing."

As Bronson described the ways anger played out in his home, it was quite evident that there was little love associated with their communication of emotions. Dr. Minirth realized that there were numerous ways that Bronson's family mismanaged their anger, and he wanted to teach them to communicate it constructively. Knowing that godly love could be real even in strong disagreements, he wanted Bronson to understand that he could guide his children in a better way of conflict resolution. He wanted Bronson to use moments of conflict to illustrate that godly love was so powerful it could even be evident amid tension. Before they could go in a positive direction, though, he and his family would need to be keenly aware of the options they were choosing that were getting them nowhere fast. By recognizing that they were choosing their misguided methods of handling anger, they could realize the individual responsibility involved in handling anger correctly.

Choices That Don't Work

Your parenting methods can be more effective as you are able to identify how both you and your children respond when you feel frustrated, annoyed, and irritated. By recognizing the patterns that take you in the direction of increased tension, you can then become ready to move on toward more productive choices.

In general, there are three common patterns that we see when people misuse anger: suppression, open aggression, and passive-aggressive anger. Let's look at each of these patterns carefully for the purpose of clarifying how anger can become problematic.

Suppressing Anger

Most people have concluded that anger can be a painful and destructive emotion. Having been involved in circumstances where anger exposed the worst in personalities, many people resolve that they will not let their anger go to ugly extremes. The result is suppression of anger. When people suppress anger, they either do not want to admit or do not want to expose their anger. They have determined that the best way to avoid the harmful fallout of anger is to keep it from ever being shown.

When do you make the determination that it would be wisest not to show your anger at all? (For instance, "I never want my children to see me flustered, so I work hard not to let them know when they are getting to me," or "My husband is so overbearing with his anger that I feel I've got to keep the calm at home.")

_____

_____

_____

When do you notice that your children suppress anger? (For instance, "My son keeps everything to himself. He hates to let anyone think there's anything wrong," or "My daughter doesn't really let people get close.")

_____

_____

_____

To get an idea of how common the suppression of anger can be among your family members, look over this list of characteristics that accompany the pattern. You might place the initials of the family members next to the statements that apply to each person.

_____ Not inclined to initiate conversation about conflictual topics
_____ Being image-conscious, wanting to appear "together"
_____ A reluctance to be direct about hurts or needs
_____ Deliberately avoiding conflict
_____ Hiding feelings of confusion or hurt
_____ Being reserved about discussing personal topics
_____ Letting hours, or even days, go by before telling anyone about a hurt
_____ A tendency to be depressive or sullen
_____ Holding onto resentments that others may never know about
_____ Appeasing others in the hope of making conflict go away
_____ Doubting the validity of personal opinions or perceptions
_____ Feeling paralyzed when confronted with an unwanted situation

If you or your child can relate to at least five of these statements, there is a strong probability that a pattern of suppression is in place. The short-term result of choosing this path can be avoidance of tension. The long-term result of this choice is an ever increasing propensity toward depression, anxiety, and chronic disillusionment.

In what circumstances do you find yourself suppressing anger? (For instance, "When more than one family member is angry, I may pretend that I'm feeling calm and collected when I really am not," or "I'm a conflict-avoider and I'll do anything to stay out of an argument.")

_____

_____

_____

In what circumstances do your children seem to suppress their anger? (For instance, "My daughter will never let her friends know that she feels hurt," or "When I try to discuss conflicts with my son, he tries to let on that it's no big deal, even though I know better.")

_____

_____

_____

In Bronson's family, he rarely suppressed. "I don't do a good job of just letting things ride," he explained. "When I'm miffed the whole house knows it." His wife, Carol, and their eight-year-old, Carissa, were a different story. "Carol has told me a hundred times that she won't fight with me, and she means it. The minute I go into one of my anger spells, she shuts down. I could plead with her for a week, but she won't talk. Her father was pretty loud, just like me, so I think she's concluded that nothing good will ever come of any discussion about problems."

Dr. Minirth probed, "And Carissa has her mother's tendency?"

"Absolutely!" came the reply. "She has her mother's same soft temperament, so she's not inclined toward loud behavior anyway. Also, having two strong-willed older brothers doesn't give her much incentive to come out into the open with her feelings. They love her as a little sister, but they've also made it perfectly clear where she stands in the pecking order."

"When Carol or Carissa hold in their feelings, how does this affect the rest of you?"

"Well, the boys don't seem to be too affected by it since it means they have that much less competition for the floor. But me, I hate it when someone holds back, especially when it's Carol. I know she's got to be feeling *something*, and it drives me crazy when she won't just get it out in the open."

How about your family? What tends to happen when one or more members suppress anger? (For instance, "We sometimes let problems quietly build; then it finally comes out in a major eruption," or "Feelings of discouragement and resentment just build.")

_____

_____

_____

Suppression of anger is a choice. Keep in mind that it does little to ultimately resolve anyone's struggle with anger. Though the anger is not revealed raucously, it does not dissolve if it is quietly harbored. Suppression represents a form of pain avoidance, which is not necessarily a wrong desire. But because it tends to feed depressive and disillusioned feelings, it only ensures that the pain will be experienced at a later date. The positive results of suppression are short-lived.

As a contrast, Galatians 6:2 teaches that we are to "bear one another's burdens, and thus fulfill the law of Christ." It was written in the context of confronting a fellow believer who is struggling with sin. The implication of this teaching is that openness is preferred in circumstances where others are struggling. We need each other to help bring perspective to our problems, and it is good to become proactively involved when problems occur. Suppressing anger works directly against this approach. Ideally, families are to be a safe haven where life lessons can be experienced. When parents indicate that they openly encourage safe exposure of emotions, they are laying the groundwork for effective life skills useful in many other relationships and circumstances.

Openly Aggressive Anger

When most people think of misapplied anger, it is openly aggressive anger that comes first to mind. True to the nature of anger, it is experienced when you want to preserve worth, needs, and convictions, but it is communicated in a manner that shows little or no regard for the needs of the other persons involved. The anger may begin for a legitimate reason, but that legitimacy can be completely missed as others feel demeaned or devalued. Primary to this form of anger is the lack of love that accompanies it. Ultimately it detracts from the spiritual vitality of the home.

This category of anger can include explosiveness, rage, and intimidation, but it is not limited to these extreme forms of expression. It can also include griping, bickering, and whining. To get an idea of the level of aggressive anger in your home, look over these descriptions of aggressive anger. Next to each description, you might place the initials of the family members who use anger in that fashion.

_____ Blunt and abrasive speech
_____ Physically abusive behavior, like shoving or throwing things
_____ Deeply insulting words, use of foul language
_____ Asking loaded questions for the purpose of demeaning the other person ("What's wrong with you?" "Why do you have to be so disagreeable?")
_____ Speaking words of accusation or blame
_____ Repeating key ideas as the conversation unfolds
_____ Open defiance and lack of cooperation
_____ Being critical as opinions are expressed
_____ Forcefully speaking rebuttals or denials
_____ Being strong-willed, pushing your agenda
_____ Speaking with an annoyed tone of voice
_____ Maintaining a condescending spirit as a conflict proceeds
_____ Being argumentative
_____ Being strongly insistent or bossy
_____ Bickering, and other forms of snippy communication

_____ Easily commenting on what is wrong with people and circumstances

There are certainly other ways anger can be managed aggressively, but this list should give you an idea of its manifestations. If you or your children can relate to five or more of these choices, there is a strong likelihood that anger can be explosive in your home.

What forms of aggressive anger are you most prone to? (For instance, "I can be patient for a while; then I'll start backing my daughter into a corner with accusing questions," or "I've got a short fuse and I can pop off with irritable statements easily.")

_____

_____

_____

What about your children? How do they express anger aggressively? (For instance, "My teenager is openly defiant and refuses to cooperate with all sorts of house rules," or "My daughter will openly confront me when I tell her something she doesn't like to hear.")

_____

_____

_____

What seems to trigger the aggression most easily in your home? (For instance, "I'm orderly in the way I keep my home cleaned, and I can't tolerate laziness and sloppiness," or "We have constant schedule conflicts among our family members, and it's very common for us to gripe about the inconvenience this poses.")

_____

_____

_____

Bronson had no difficulty identifying his own tendency to be openly aggressive in expressing his anger "I guess there's no question that I set the pace for aggressiveness in my family. I've lectured myself constantly about how I shouldn't let things get to me, but one of my sons can show just the slightest amount of disrespect and I'm all over him."

"What do you hope to accomplish when you use the overpowering approach?" Dr. Minirth asked.

"Oh, I've never really thought about it on a deep level, but I guess it's my way of letting the other person know that I *will* be taken seriously."

"Does it work?"

A look of frustration crossed Bronson's face as he slowly shook his head. "No, I can't say that it does. Maybe for a short while I can force some compliance, but this has been going on for years and my family is sick of all the fighting. I can feel that I'm losing them one by one. Carol and I have a strained relationship most of the time, and it's obvious to the kids that we're rarely in synch. Jonathan, in particular, seems to have suffered the most from my tirades. Being the oldest, he's probably caught more of my reprimands than the other two. There are times when I think he hates me just like I used to hate my own father."

Ephesians 4:29 instructs: "Let no unwholesome word proceed from your mouth, but only such a word as is good for edification according to the need of the moment." This is one more passage that underscores the thought that there can be moments when problems need to be openly addressed, but it clearly recognizes the debilitating effects of unedifying communication. In the short run, forceful anger may serve the purpose of forcing compliance or of venting frustrations, but over the course of time there is little to be gained by such an approach.

Think about the moments when you express your anger aggressively. What are you trying to accomplish with an overpowering approach? (For instance, "I want my son to know without a doubt that my word is final," or "I've got to raise the decibels because that's the only way I'll be taken seriously.")

Consider also why your children may communicate with aggression. Why do you suppose they use this method? (For instance, "My daughter begins every conflict with the assumption that she won't be heard; she's very pessimistic," or "My son has learned that he can get his way if he pitches a fit.")

_____

_____

_____

When people use aggressive anger, it is generally accompanied by the pessimistic assumption that listening will not occur unless force is involved. Aggressive people have concluded, sometimes with good reason, that others do not really care to make room for a thought or idea that is different from their own. As a result, they assume the only way to have their needs addressed is to show strength, even if it is a bully's form of strength.

If you think carefully about the attitude of an aggressive person, you can easily find that insecurity and uncertainty push it along. Though the aggressive person may sound strong and powerful, behind the forcefulness is a fear that harmony probably cannot be found through a calmer manner of speech or behavior.

How is your aggression or the aggression of your child a signal of insecurity? (For instance, "In our family it seems that no one is committed to listening, and that has an unsettling effect," or "My son is so accustomed to hearing his parents argue that he's determined that no one really cares about the other unless forced to do so.")

_____

_____

_____

Let's be as practical as possible in determining the effects of aggressive anger. Think carefully: Does it work? Bronson was forced to admit that his influence in the lives of his children had decreased steadily over the years. Jonathan and Cody had developed the habit of either bickering openly with him or withdrawing altogether. Predictably, they concluded that their dad was a pain, so they anticipated friction even when it was not necessarily forthcoming.

What response do you receive when you are too aggressive? (For instance, "Our house has constant tension because we've all come to expect explosions," or "My kids feel so pessimistic about their home life that they've just quit trying to be cordial.")

_____

_____

_____

Let's reiterate that aggressive anger may be spurred by reasonable thoughts, but once others realize that you are withholding respect the reasonable message is lost. In the short run, you may coerce some compliance, but over the course of time this option will lead to a home atmosphere of chronic defeat and pessimism.

Passive-Aggressive Anger

Some people express their anger in a way that creates frustration and disharmony, but without being openly belligerent. They use passive-aggressive anger. True to the definition of anger, they wish to preserve personal worth, needs, and convictions, but the aggressive element is less overt. Their protest is more likely to be displayed through quiet nonparticipation or behind-the-scenes sabotage. Usually, people using passive-aggressive anger have concluded that they cannot win an argument with open force, so they use evasiveness or an unapproachable spirit to make their gain.

To recognize passive-aggressive anger, look over this list of qualities common to the pattern. You will notice that in each behavior there is a form of self-preservation at someone else's expense, but it is managed so that the angry person has the least amount of emotional exposure. Next to each trait, you might place the initials of the family member who fits its description.

_____ Ignoring people or tuning others out
_____ Chronic forgetfulness or not following through on promises
_____ Laziness and procrastination

_____ Quietly doing what pleases oneself while disregarding others'
wishes

_____ Being unreliable in following through on tasks

_____ Telling others what they want to hear, with no intention of
actually doing what is said

_____ Appearing cooperative, but behind the scenes being uncooperative

_____ Doing things with timing that does not factor in the needs of
others

_____ Chronic tardiness, waiting until the last minute to get things done

_____ Becoming stone silent in conflict

_____ Approaching work tasks half-heartedly

_____ Being evasive

There are other ways passive-aggressive anger can be shown, but these
should give you an idea of how people act when they do not want to be
vulnerable in experiencing anger. If you can relate to five or more of
these behaviors, there is a strong likelihood that passive-aggressiveness
is an ongoing part of your relating style.

Bronson recognized that he had a very low inclination toward passive-
aggressive anger. "Sometimes I'll withdraw and pout, so I guess that might
fit your description," he told Dr. Minirth. "But I can easily see how my
son Cody and Carol do this a lot."

At fourteen, Cody was known as the one in the family who was hardest
to reach. When he was home he stayed to himself, and he rarely showed
his emotions in a loud fashion. "Most of the time he parks in front of
the TV, and when I try to talk with him, he just barely acknowledges my
presence," Bronson explained. "When he and Jonathan get into arguments, he's capable of throwing some stinging zingers, but most of the
time he won't look at anyone, and he makes it his business to be as mini-
mally involved as he can."

"How does this affect the rest of the family's mood?"

"Well, Carol is kind of similar to Cody in the way she acts. In fact,
I think the two feed off of one another. She's the kind of person who will
give the silent treatment when she's ticked. She has gone as long as a week
without saying one word to me. I swear, it drives me crazy and it makes
the house feel very tense. Usually I don't respond well to either one of

them when they do the withdrawal thing. I think they know how much it bothers me, which motivates them more to continue in that style."

Bronson was onto something with his observation. Passive-aggressive people may not play their cards openly, but they know exactly what they are doing. Feeling unappreciated or disgruntled with their relationships, their life can become a quiet protest against the things they do not like. In passivity, their self-protective message is, "You're not going to bother me without having to pay a price for it."

How do you express your anger with passive-aggressiveness? (For instance, "I know when my family members need help in their chores, but I'll make myself unavailable," or "I'll give my kids a glare, but I won't actually say what is bothering me.")

_____

_____

_____

How do your children display passive-aggressive anger? (For instance, "My daughter tells me she's done her homework, but I'll find the assignments completely undone," or "My son tells me he'll be out with a clean-cut kid; then I learn later that he was running around with the one person I've told him to stay away from.")

_____

_____

_____

Passive-aggressiveness is characterized by fear. People who use anger this way have determined that any open exposure of feelings and needs is met with a rebuke, and they assume that the effort to openly assert their convictions will be painful. In the effort to avoid that pain, they choose to be subtler in displaying their anger. Being passive allows them to avoid being vulnerable in their anger, even as they get their anger message out.

As an example, when Bronson yelled at his son Cody, the lad would often retreat to his bedroom and stay for hours, speaking to no one.

Later if Bronson accused him of being "out of it," Cody would look at him incredulously and say, "Dad, I was just listening to music in my room. That's all I was doing." Cody might not finish the rest of his message, which would have been, "Dad, I find you to be an offensive person and I need to keep my distance from you." His fear would not allow him to be that honest.

When you act passive-aggressively, what are you afraid of at that moment? (For instance, "I fear looking stupid if my family knew why I was really hurting," or "I fear the rejection that's so predictable when I let my needs be known.")

_____

_____

_____

When your children act passive-aggressively, what do you suppose they are afraid of? (For instance, "My daughter fears that honesty can bring a harsh response from me," or "My son is afraid of looking weak if he exposes what he really feels.")

_____

_____

_____

In addition to fear, passive-aggressive anger is driven by the craving for power. We think of openly aggressive persons as the ones who wield the most power since their manner can be so forceful. Yet, it is the passive-aggressive person who ultimately controls the relationship. Whereas the openly aggressive style of anger insists on action now, the use of passive-aggressiveness indicates, "I do things in my own timing. If you think you're going to run my life, I've got a message for you . . . it won't work." Unlike open aggression, passive-aggressive behavior is accompanied by quiet stubbornness, meaning that the angry person can act disruptively but then deny that he or she is being obstinate.

Cody had the misfortune of having an older brother who bullied him often and a dad who was so quick with his anger that he (Cody) knew he would never be heard. Even though he did not plan consciously to become a passive-aggressive respondent, that is exactly what happened over the course of time. He once confided to his mother, "Dad and Jonathan think they can just snap their fingers and I'll do whatever they want. I'm sick of living like I'm their slave. I'm just going to do what I want to do and if they don't like it, that's tough."

Can you see that in his anger, Cody was attempting to preserve his worth, his needs, his convictions? At the base of his fuming emotions was a reasonable desire to be treated with dignity. He had learned early in life, though, that it would do no good to be open about such matters, but his drive for respect would not allow him to take no action of self-preservation. Knowing he could not win if he went head to head with his dad or his brother, he developed the sly manner of showing them up with stubborn resistance. It gave him a feeling of power.

When you use passive-aggressive anger, what power message are you sending? (For instance, "I'm letting my kids know that there's a price to pay if they try to mess with me," or "It's my way of indicating that I won't play their games.")

_____

_____

_____

When your children display passive-aggressiveness toward you, what power message are they communicating? (For instance, "I'll do what I want to do, when I want to do it," or "I'll look cooperative on the outside, but you can't touch how I feel on the inside.")

_____

_____

_____

Assessing the Damage

So far we have identified three ways anger can be managed in your home. You can suppress it. You can be openly aggressive with it. You can be passive-aggressive. It is important to remember that each of these methods is a choice. They are lousy choices; nonetheless, you can opt for them if that is what you want.

Accompanying each of these forms of anger management is futility. Simply put, if you choose to handle your anger in a poor manner, you will get poor results. As you make unhealthy choices in your own anger management, your children will do the same.

Part of the role of parents is to teach. (Our word *discipline* is derived from a Greek root word meaning "to teach.") We want to encourage you to think of yourself as a professor preparing your young for the emotional twists and turns of family life. Before you can expect your children to learn from your instructions, it would be best if you first display a willingness to set aside the choice to mismanage anger, opting instead for better alternatives. The best way to teach is not through verbal instruction, but through modeling. As you illustrate that an emotion such as anger does little other than generate feelings of discord or bitterness, you have low credibility when you later attempt to teach your kids about kindness, forgiveness, or respect. Children take their cues from their authority figures, so as the parents get a handle on the best ways to address anger they have credibility once they go into a broader instruction mode with their kids.

As you take inventory of the aspects of your anger that go awry, what stands out as the most prominent feature in need of adjustment? (For instance, "I need to gripe less and speak more in an even tone of voice," or "Rather than making others squirm with my silence, I need to be more forthcoming with what I really feel.")

_____

_____

_____

Dr. Minirth explained to Bronson, "At times I'm sure you feel pretty frustrated as you see how the various family members handle their anger poorly. I want you to use this time to reflect on how you can positively affect your family's future as you make a concerted effort to shift gears in the way you manage your emotions."

Bronson had a look of defeat as he shook his head: "I don't know if my family will even listen to me at this point. We're so accustomed to having friction that it's just become a way of life for all of us."

"You can choose to stay on the same course if that's what you like," replied the doctor. "Right now, recognize that you have everything to gain as you shift gears and learn how to be more appropriate in addressing conflict. The one thing that determines if you can help your family turn over a new leaf is your willpower."

The same is true for you. We encourage you to become honest about how anger is mishandled in your home for the purpose of spurring you toward a better way. In the next chapter, we concentrate on some of the better choices you can make as you address anger with your children.

For Family Discussion

Let's walk through each of the methods of handling anger that have been identified in this chapter:

1. Have each family member identify two or three incidents when he or she chose to suppress anger. Why does he or she make such a choice?

2. Have family members identify how they might communicate anger with open aggression. At the moment of anger, why do they choose to communicate their feelings in this fashion?

3. Have each family member identify two or three incidents of choosing to be passive-aggressive with his or her anger. What is the "advantage" of this style of anger?

4. Go around the room and have each person identify healthier ways of choosing to communicate anger. At this point, it would be appropriate for each family member to offer suggestions to one another regarding the preferred changes.

5. Have each family member respond to the question, "Why is it so essential to acknowledge that your style of anger is the result of a specific choice?"

For Further Reflection

Ephesians 6:4 says: "Fathers, do not provoke your children to anger, but bring them up in the discipline and instruction of the Lord."

1. What causes parents to be provoked by their children to the extent that they may struggle to discipline their children appropriately?

2. What is the quickest way for you to provoke your children to anger? What are you attempting to accomplish as you behave this way?

3. How might your suppression of anger actually keep the atmosphere of anger alive in your home? When it is clear that your children are suppressing, what are they attempting to communicate to you?

Proverbs 29:22 states: "An angry man stirs up strife and a hot tempered man abounds in aggression."

4. How does your openly aggressive use of anger stir up strife in your children? Why do you choose this method of anger communication?

5. When do you use passively aggressive forms of anger? How does this in turn provoke anger in your children?

James 5:16 indicates: "Confess your sins to one another, and pray for one another so that you may be healed."

6. How do parents establish leadership within the home when they confess their poor use of anger? How do their children tend to respond when the parent confesses sinful anger?

7. What would be different in your home if you regularly prayed regarding how each family member handles anger?

3

HEALTHY WAYS TO MANAGE ANGER

STEP 3: When you have a responsible message to communicate, do so in a way that upholds the dignity of the others involved.

Parents often ask, "Do I have the right to be angry with my kids?" These adults realize that it is sometimes impossible *not* to feel agitated when their children are disruptive and contrary. They want to learn if it is reasonable to let their children know how angry they are.

To put a different perspective on the subject, we ask the parents to make a slight adjustment in their line of questioning. "Take the word *right* and throw it away," we say. "When you think only in terms of your rights, your focus is singular, since you are concerned only about what is good for yourself. Replace it with the word *responsibility*, and then ask the question again."

"Do I have a responsibility to be angry with my kids?" This question has a different slant. Instead of focusing only on what is best for yourself, you can focus on what is best for both yourself and your children. You can be challenged to determine if communicating anger is indeed a responsibility, not just a right.

What do you think? Is it ever responsible to communicate anger toward your children? (For instance, "Anger has been so frequently misapplied in our home that I don't really see it as a responsibility," or "It's reasonable to teach my children to factor in the needs and feelings of other family members, even my needs.")

Conflict is reality, meaning that anger in the home is reality. You do your children a disservice by not exposing them to the truth that family members can act in a way that creates frustration in one another. It is reasonable, then, for them to know that you can feel anger, just as it is reasonable to coach them to know that they too can feel anger. Your task is to help them recognize how anger can be managed most profitably.

In the first chapter, we referred to Ephesians 4:26, which states that we can be angry without sin. In verses 31–32 of the same chapter, we receive further clarification: "Let all bitterness and wrath and anger and clamor and slander be put away from you, along with all malice. And be kind to one another, tenderhearted, forgiving one another, just as God in Christ has forgiven you." The anger associated with a disrespectful spirit is to be removed in favor of such higher priorities as kindness, tenderness, and forgiveness. Healthy anger can still be communicated, but it can be accomplished within the context of those higher priorities.

When we work with parents like Bronson and his wife, Carol, we want them to know that anger can be mobilized in a way that can lead to good results. Dr. Minirth explained to Bronson: "You've developed such a reputation as a harsh person that it's going to take a major effort on your part to regain your positive influence with your three children." Bronson frowned as he realized just how true the statement was. The doctor continued: "Don't give up in discouragement, though. Think of how impressed your children will be when they recognize that you're learning to turn away from your previous aggressive anger. I'm hoping they'll take note of your better choices and eventually join you in the effort. Are you up to it?"

Bronson's children were weary of his anger, but it was equally true that *he* was weary of his own anger. He had long recognized that his children were slipping away from him. So, yes, he was ready to try something different.

Think for a moment about why you would want to improve how you manage your anger with your children. What is your motive behind the desire for change? (For instance, "I don't want my children to be defensive around me; I like the idea of openness in our home," or "If I'm going to ask my son to get a grip on his anger, I need to lead the way by example.")

_____

_____

_____

The Better Alternative

To get an idea of how to begin restructuring your anger so it will have a more constructive outcome, it is good to focus on the theme of speaking the truth in love. When you have anger toward your children, most of the time there is a truth that you wish to convey. Your anger may be spurred by the truths that sharing is better than fighting; telling lies will lead nowhere; sassing is not a good way to speak to your elders; it is best to be timely in performing chores. If your child has provoked you with anger, it is usually a signal that they need to hear truth from you.

Ask yourself, _Do I speak truth in love?_ Most people do not associate anger with love. Assuming that anger is a crass, pain-producing emotion, it is easy to think of anger as a nonloving reaction. Healthy anger, though, can actually enhance the possibility of creating a more loving home environment.

When your child is disobedient or smart-alecky or tuned out, how loving do you feel at that moment? You probably don't have warm, fuzzy emotions in the face of such rude behavior. Think carefully though. Is it loving _not_ to address the problem at hand? No! To allow your children to continue in poor behavior is to enable dysfunctional habits. No loving parent wants to do that. It is your love for your children that prompts you to address wrongs.

What loving motive do you have as you feel the need to express your frustrations with your children? (For instance, "My love for my son is what makes me address the issue of his alcohol use," or "Because I love my daughter, I want her to learn that respectfulness is the best path to take in her communication style.")

_____

_____

_____

Can you learn to communicate your loving motive in a manner that keeps your anger from becoming ugly and counterproductive? That's the question Dr. Minirth posed to Bronson.

"I can honestly say that I've never learned to put love and anger together on the same side of the page," he admitted. "That's a whole new idea for me to ponder."

Assertive Anger

To communicate anger in a way that remains consistent with your motives of love, you need to commit to assertiveness. Some people have assumed that assertiveness means they should say whatever they want to say to get their own way; if others don't like what they have to say, that's their problem. Such a brash manner of communication is not assertiveness at all.

Assertive anger is defined as the willingness to preserve your worth, needs, and convictions while also being fully respectful of the other people involved. Just as you want to be valued as a person of dignity, you will demonstrate the same dignity outwardly.

To get an idea of how assertiveness can be expressed, look over this list of behaviors. You might place the family members' initials next to the ones that need most attention.

_____ Speaking confidently while also remaining calm
_____ Being specific, as opposed to vague or general, about your unmet needs

_____ Knowing when to say no, and being firm in that decision
_____ Talking about difficult issues in a respectful tone of voice
_____ Following through on what is right, even when there is opposition
_____ Sticking to good plans, instead of being talked into less wise decisions
_____ Clearly explaining what you can and cannot do; setting boundaries
_____ Following through with fair consequences when necessary
_____ Being immediate in addressing problems, as opposed to letting them simmer
_____ Remaining consistent in your convictions

How can you do a better job of communicating your anger assertively? (For instance, "I tend to tell my daughter that she'll have to pay consequences, but then I don't follow through," or "My son can be so belligerent that I just won't address our issues anymore.")

_____

_____

_____

How about your kids? How would they benefit by learning to be properly assertive? (For instance, "My daughter needs to learn how to be firmer in her convictions with a girlfriend who is very forceful," or "My son needs to know he can speak up when he's upset instead of holding his anger in.")

_____

_____

_____

To Bronson's credit, he decided it was time for a change. He recognized that the good ideas he wanted his children to hear were lost in his brash way of communicating anger. After several counseling sessions that challenged him to try a new approach, he found an opportunity to channel his anger differently. He walked in the back door one evening as Jonathan was clearly making life miserable for his younger brother. Normally it would have thrown Dad into a tirade, but this time he spoke calmly: "Looks to me like you're not having a very good afternoon. Jonathan, tell me why you're feeling so upset with your brother."

Predictably, Jonathan went into the blame mode. "I told Cody to never get stuff out of my room without asking first. Here he is, though, using my new CD and he never once thought to check with me about it." His voice was shrill and his face was full of tension.

Cody shot back: "When I walked into the den, the CD was already in the CD player, so I just turned it on and listened to it. Jonathan had no intention of listening to it because he was in his room doing something else. What's the big deal? Can't he share?"

The boys bickered a little longer, but for once Bronson did not enter the fray. Calmly he said, "Jonathan, I see nothing wrong with Cody listening to your CD, particularly since it was already in the boom box and you had no plans to use it." Then turning to Cody, he said, "You know that you tend to make a big deal when your brother uses something of yours without asking. If he insists, let him have the CD and just get one of your own to play instead." He was even-keeled as he spoke.

When he told Dr. Minirth about this simple incident, the doctor replied, "That's exactly the way I hope you can handle your anger— more cleanly. Say what needs to be said, and then let your sons take it from there."

"Well, before you congratulate me, let me tell you what happened next. Jonathan decided he wouldn't let Cody listen to his CD, so he ripped the CD case out of his brother's hand, took the CD out of the player, and began to storm out of the room. Cody was ticked, and so was I. Before you knew it, I grabbed Jonathan by the arm and started lecturing him about his attitude. He just jerked away from me and left. I was in a miserable mood the rest of the night."

Bronson had begun his anger communication with a loving motive. He wanted his sons to learn the value of fair play. He had even communicated his conviction in a respectful tone of voice. His sons, Jonathan in particular, still wanted nothing to do with this friendlier assertion, so he responded poorly.

When have you tried to be respectful in addressing a frustration with your child, only to be greeted with a poor reaction? (For instance, "Last night I calmly spoke to my daughter about the need to get her dirty clothes off the bathroom floor, and she just went into a huff," or "When I address my needs with my son, he just rolls his eyes at me.")

_____

_____

_____

How does this undesirable response affect you? (For instance, "I'm doing all I can not to let it rip," or "I start lecturing.")

_____

_____

_____

Let's acknowledge that when you attempt to manage your anger fairly, there is no guarantee that your child will respond with an appreciative attitude. When you call your children down for a wrong behavior, they can feel humiliation, even if it is not warranted. Your reprimand may be a reminder that they are not allowed to get away with raw selfishness or gross disregard for family members. In immaturity, they may give you a poor response, and at that moment your challenge is to remain in a mode of respect.

"That's where I usually get pulled into a wrong anger response," Bronson confessed. "I expect that when I say something it had better be taken seriously."

"There's nothing wrong with that desire," came the doctor's reply. "Let's keep in mind that right now, and maybe for some time, you're ahead of them as you try to come to terms with the issue of anger. You'll need patience as you work on keeping your assertive communication from crossing the line into aggressiveness."

One of the biggest mistakes you can make as you communicate your anger assertively is to assume that your effort should be met with a co-operative response. Make room for the possibility that your child will protest, or that you will sense disagreement. Even as the child responds poorly, you can stay your course. Remember, the healthy goal of anger is preserving legitimate needs and convictions. It does not include force-feeding those same desires. Don't be shocked if your child remains in a surly disposition.

I Peter 3:9 indicates that we are not to return "evil for evil or insult for insult"; it further indicates that we are to give "a blessing instead." This puts a heavy responsibility on the parents' shoulders not to become drawn into the childish or adversarial style of anger that is so common in a moment of conflict. As you choose the assertive approach to anger, make room for the possibility that you might not be well received, and brace yourself to maintain your composure if there is a meltdown or stormy protest. In doing so, you establish leadership.

How can your anger be contained if you are less shocked by your child's undesirable response to your clean assertions? (For instance, "I'd be willing to listen more and talk less," or "I would remember that I didn't always respond wonderfully to my own parents' requests when I was the same age.")

_____

_____

_____

If your children do not respond well to your anger, you still have two options: you can use the "nonetheless" approach, or you can calmly apply consequences.

"Nonetheless"

Bronson's sons did not respond well when he tried to play referee in their dispute over the use of Jonathan's CD. Once Jonathan left the room, Cody was the first to air his displeasure: "Every time I do something that he doesn't like, he's always ready to pounce. He's the biggest jerk I know."

At this point, it would be fair for Bronson to gently reiterate what he had said earlier: "Even though you don't agree with Jonathan's response, it's fair for you to ask him if you can use what belongs to him, just as you'd like to have him do the same in reverse."

Let's suppose, though, that Cody does not buy his dad's reasoning. He continues complaining. At that point, Bronson can choose to erupt, or he can calmly state, "I know you're upset; nonetheless, it's reasonable to check with him first when you want to use his things."

Let's further speculate that Cody *still* is not satisfied and repeats his complaint yet another time. Bronson can once again state, "Nonetheless, it's reasonable to check with him first."

As Dr. Minirth talked with Bronson about holding his ground calmly without becoming aggressive, Bronson admitted, "That would be very unnatural for me."

The doctor explained, "When kids challenge parents' authority, it's very tempting to explain in no uncertain terms who the boss is. Rarely does this work, but that's what we want to do. A cleaner approach would have you stand firmly while giving your child the time to absorb the common sense that accompanies your assertiveness."

In what circumstances could you use the nonetheless approach? (For instance, "I need to calmly hold my ground when my daughter is tired late in the afternoon and is prone to emotional meltdown," or "When I'm discussing curfew with my son, I need to cease from being drawn into useless debates and calmly stick to what I know is wise.")

_____

_____

_____

What is it about the calm approach to firmness that can be most challenging to you? (For instance, "Every time my son smarts off with me, I feel the need to correct him right there on the spot," or "I feel as if my calmness might be construed as weakness.")

_____

_____

_____

When you express your anger with your children, your spirit communicates more powerfully than your actual words. Whether you realize it or not, you are constantly sending unspoken messages through your personal demeanor. When you rant and rave or speak caustically, you subtly send the message, "I'm feeling weak; you're getting to me." If you calmly hold your ground without bickering, you send the message, "I'm comfortable with my decision, and I invite you to accept what I'm saying."

Consequences

No matter how reasonable your message to your children is, and no matter how respectfully you communicate it, you still may not receive the desired response. They may continue to gripe or choose to be defiant and act contradictory to your convictions. Staying within the desire to remain assertive, you still have the option to apply consequences.

Let's first acknowledge that discussing consequences with your children is not the same as making threats. There is a subtle yet powerful distinction between applying consequences and making threats. When you threaten your children, there is a message of vengeance or coercion. It usually draws you deeper into an adversarial relationship with them. Applying consequences is not an attempt to demonstrate dominance. Instead, consequences can be driven by loving motives as you show your children how the real world works. You are teaching that an uncooperative or selfish motive brings an unpleasant result. The earlier the child can learn such a lesson, the more successful he or she will be in all relationships.

One of Bronson's pet peeves as a parent was his kids' tendency to be lax in keeping their portion of the house clean. "Carol and I are on their backs constantly, but it never dawns on them to take the initiative themselves," he explained to the doctor. "We have arguments almost daily about who's supposed to clean what."

"How do you manage your anger during those moments?"

"Being honest, I start with an attitude of frustration," Bronson admitted, "and when I get the predictable back talk, that frustration comes out for all to see."

If parents extend too much effort jousting with their children in frustration, it gives the child the impression that the parent is feeling out of control. Playing upon that feeling, the child can feel empowered to remain stubborn or uncooperative. Instead of seeing the parent as someone to take seriously, the children can remain in the adversarial position indefinitely, feeling empowered by the prospect of wearing down the resolve of the parents.

Have you ever noticed how your children repeatedly fail to take your requests seriously, even after you plead with them to be cooperative? How does this play out in your home? (For instance, "Every day it's a fight to get my daughter to practice her music," or "My kids constantly gripe when I ask for help doing common household chores.")

_____

_____

_____

As you commit yourself to a clean, assertive means of managing anger, you can opt out of circular arguments. Instead, you can tell your children what you expect from them, and then if they choose to argue or disobey you can calmly explain the consequences for lack of compliance. At that point, you need say no more.

For instance, if Bronson or Carol receive griping as they ask their three kids to help clean the house, they can respond with consequences, not condescension. "If you continue complaining about the chores or if you choose not to do them," they can explain, "the consequence is the loss of television and computer privileges for the rest of the day. It's up to you." If the kids give a predictable whining response, they can reply, "Nonetheless, that's the consequence. You get to decide how you'd like to handle this."

In what circumstances do you need to argue less with your children, applying consequences instead? (For instance, "Each morning when my son is late for school, I can quit begging him to be on time; if he has to serve a detention after school, that will be his choice," or "Instead of arguing about the clothes my daughter wants to wear, I can establish a reasonable guideline and let her know that if she chooses to contradict me then social privileges will be withdrawn.")

_____

_____

_____

When speaking to your child about consequences, there are two guidelines to follow:

1. Be sure the consequence is reasonable. Being excessive only creates defeat and can cause the child to refuse to be cooperative.
2. The consequence needs to be spoken in a plain, even tone of voice, not in a threatening manner. Stick to the facts rather than trying to intimidate your child into submission.

When you use consequences as part of your assertiveness, your goal need not be to make the young person feel terrific about your directions. (Did *you* always agree with everything your parents said to you?) Instead, the calm yet firm statement of consequences indicates that you believe in what you are saying, so there is no need to beg the child to agree.

List three or four recurring conflicts in your home that probably need to be met with consequences. (For instance, "Telling lies," or "Missing curfew," or "Smoking cigarettes.")

_____

_____

_____

Now go back through each of the conflicts you have just listed and determine a fair consequence for that behavior. (For instance, "Loss of money," or "Staying in for the weekend," or "Loss of computer privileges.")

_____

_____

_____

Releasing Anger

Once you establish a habit of speaking your assertions with respect and applying consequences with calm firmness, you are well on your way to significantly reducing the level of anger in the home. Even so, there can still be circumstances with your children that continue to provoke your anger. Your challenge is to maintain a respectful demeanor, even though you may feel like giving in to your anger.

Consider some sobering thoughts about the nature of children:

_____ No matter how many times you talk with them about maintaining a cooperative attitude, they can still forget to cooperate.
_____ Griping and whining can be first nature to children. It's part of their immaturity.
_____ Not all children are self-motivated.
_____ Just as adults can be self-centered, children can exhibit this trait too.
_____ Even when you are using crystal clear logic, it may not make sense to the young person.

Whenever you encounter the parts of your children that seem permanently out of balance with your thinking, you are at a fork in the road. Do you continue to use assertive anger in the hope that the child will change, or do you just accept the imperfection and move on?

There are times it is wise to know when not to act upon your anger at all. Recall that Ephesians 4:31–32 indicates that you can put away the ugly forms of anger as you choose instead to maintain a spirit of kindness, tenderness, and forgiveness. You can determine to let go of the anger so you can focus on such priorities. This is what we refer to as releasing anger. By releasing your anger, you recognize that there are other, more important traits you want to emphasize in your role as a parent. Releasing anger involves various choices:

_____ Accepting the child despite weaknesses or flaws
_____ Maintaining an overall reputation as an encourager, not a critic
_____ Maintaining expectations consistent with the child's maturity level
_____ Choosing to forgive, even if it has not been earned
_____ Picking your battles carefully, refusing to get into minor skirmishes
_____ Letting kindness be a dominant trait, even as you discipline
_____ Accepting the reality that your child does not always want to hear your opinion

_____ Choosing patience because that's what you want to be known for

_____ Sidestepping the temptation to bicker or to keep pressing your point

_____ Allowing your child to have a perception that is different from yours

By choosing to release your anger, you affirm that you do not want anger to be the primary trait in your role as parent. You recognize that there are many possibilities to express anger but you will focus only on the circumstances that truly need your attention. You affirm that you want your child to know you have plenty of acceptance to offer, even when he or she proves to be different or imperfect.

In what situations do you need to choose to release your anger? (For instance, "When my daughter says she hates the way she looks, I don't need to comment and then get drawn into an argument," or "Once I've explained our financial limits to my son, if he wants to feel sorry for himself I can resist the temptation to scold him for what he feels.")

_____

_____

_____

What is it about releasing your anger that is difficult or unnatural? (For instance, "I like matters to be tied down, so letting things slide is hard for me," or "When I display acceptance, I run the risk of my son interpreting it as condoning.")

_____

_____

_____

Carol's personality was fairly mellow, so it was not difficult for her to examine how she could improve her relations with her children by letting go of some anger opportunities. Bronson, however, had to stretch his mind to make room for the possibility of releasing anger. "Do you realize how hard that'll be for me?" he asked Dr. Minirth. "Part of the reason I'm so vocal with my anger is that I'm a hands-on person, and

I can't stand the thought of just walking away when I see my sons handling things poorly."

Dr. Minirth reminded him, "We've already seen that the forceful, aggressive approach doesn't work; actually it leads to increased tension at home, plus you're modeling a rotten style of anger management that the boys will imitate." Bronson nodded as the doctor continued. "Everyone gains when you choose to be respectful in communicating your anger, but let's be reasonable enough to admit that even then you won't get full compliance. That's when I think it would be wise to let it go. You'll need to admit that you are limited in how much you can influence your children. You won't get through to them 100 percent of the time."

"So you're saying I should just eat my feelings no matter how much I don't want to do that?" Bronson was assuming that releasing anger was the same as suppressing it.

"No, that's not what I'm saying. I'm assuming that you want your sons to know that you can love them even in moments of disagreement."

Suppressing anger requires a commitment to false pretenses or phoniness. When you suppress, you try to portray yourself as being something that you are not. When you release your anger, however, you choose to let other goals take center stage. Though you may still have legitimate reasons to feel frustrated, you can give higher priority at the moment to calmness, kindness, or patience. Dr. Minirth explained to Bronson, "The key to truly releasing your anger is that you want to move on to something better."

How can you know that you are releasing your anger, not just suppressing it? (For instance, "I would honestly be able to proceed with a good mood, and it wouldn't be a fake front," or "I wouldn't dwell on the things that are negative.")

_____

_____

_____

One factor common to most children is that they have not learned the skill of emotional containment. When children emote, they are prone to letting the emotion drive their behavior beyond reason. For instance, an expressive child can allow anger to result in too strong an expression of annoyance. Likewise, a suppressive child can hold in anger to the extent that it feeds a defensive system that is more powerful than necessary.

As the parent, you are in a position to show your children a better way. You can illustrate in your own emotional management style the value of moderation. By being wise enough to release your anger, you demonstrate that it is not necessary to let your emotions take you to unnecessary extremes.

As Bronson learned to keep his anger balanced, he eventually was able to discuss with his sons, particularly Jonathan, that some battles are not worth the expenditure of strong anger. Several months after beginning his efforts to bring his anger under control, Jonathan was complaining about a restriction his mother had put on him. In the past, Bronson would have shouted about his son's defiant spirit. This time, however, he told his son, "Sounds like you had a bad day. I'm sure things will improve as the week moves along." That was it! Bronson decided to bypass the chance to be forceful. Instead he chose to be a voice of reason.

True releasing of anger is next to impossible if you have not developed good skills in assertive anger, so the two forms of healthy anger go hand-in-hand. When you know that you have been reasonable in exercising assertiveness in balanced amounts, then you can feel secure that your release of anger is part of your overall gift of a loving disposition to the family. As you consider your choices in anger management, do so with the realization that your children are observing your every move. Ultimately the best way to teach them to handle anger well is to show them what a life with balanced anger looks like.

For Family Discussion

1. Begin the discussion by having each family member give a definition of healthy anger.

2. Have each person identify two or three possible incidents when he or she might need to communicate anger assertively.

3. Let each person respond to this question: When have you tried to be assertive, only to have the other person respond uncooperatively?

4. Let each person give a response to this question: When it becomes clear that another person does not agree with your assertive behavior, what will you need to do so that your anger does not become inappropriate?

5. Take turns with one family member at a time being the focus person. Have each of the other family members express how he or she would like the focus person to speak about conflict assertively.

6. Have all family members identify incidents when they would benefit from dropping their anger altogether, giving priority to acceptance.

7. With each family member giving input, discuss the value of forgiveness of one another's failings.

For Further Reflection

Ephesians 4:15 refers to Christians "speaking the truth in love." When anger is felt, there is often a truth that needs to be lovingly communicated.

1. How can you tell when your communication of anger is being handled with a loving motive? When is it apparent that love is not really your motive in anger communication?

2. What happens to you when it appears that your children do not receive your anger communication as an expression of love?

Ephesians 4:29 says: "Let no unwholesome word proceed from your mouth, but only such a word as is good for edification according to the need of the moment, that it may give grace to those who hear."

3. How do you need to alter your approach to anger so that it is not accompanied by unwholesome words? How can you be sure that your expressions of anger are truly meeting a legitimate need?

4. What is it about appropriately expressed anger that can enhance the experience of grace?

Ephesians 4:31 tells us to put away unhealthy forms of anger; then verse 32 says: "And be kind to one another, tenderhearted, forgiving one another just as God in Christ has forgiven you."

5. How can you maintain a reputation as a kind parent even while you are committed to openness regarding your anger?

6. Sometimes you must be willing to set aside your anger in favor of forgiveness toward your children. What causes this to be a difficult choice? How does a forgiving spirit bring balance to your use of assertive anger?

4

BREAKING YOUR CYCLES
OF DEPENDENCY

*STEP 4: Have a strong sense of purpose as a parent
in order to respond to anger-producing
circumstances as an initiator, not a reactor.*

Melinda was a jovial woman in her early forties. With a pleasant round face and eyes that widened whenever she spoke, she was the type of person who could put people at ease in a flash. Her fifteen-year-old son, Blake, and her eleven-year-old daughter, Lexi, were involved in several extracurricular activities, which was just fine with Melinda. She enjoyed engaging with other adults, and her children's activities provided a social outlet for her.

Observing how friendly Melinda could be, few would suspect that she had a problem with anger. Blake and Lexi were regarded as good kids, and as far as anyone knew their family life hummed along in a pleasant manner. Melinda said to Dr. Carter: "I love my kids, don't get me wrong; they're wonderful and I wouldn't trade them for anything in the world. At the same time, though, my stomach stays tied up in knots when I'm with them."

She went on to explain how Lexi was painfully slow whenever she prepared to go out, and it created highly predictable friction each time Melinda would prod her to hurry. "She's got such an attitude," Melinda complained. "I can't say the simplest word of correction to her without her popping off at me." Blake, on the other hand, was quite passive. "Around everyone else," Melinda said, "he's as charming as can be, but at home I can't get him to talk with me about anything! It would be easier breaking into Fort Knox than to get him to tell me how he feels or what he's thinking."

She sought counseling because she was having recurring episodes of anger. She told Dr. Carter, "I try to keep my cool, but each of my kids in their own unique way can push my buttons, and before you know it, I'm saying things I shouldn't say. I can get drawn into arguments way too easily." Shaking her head, she admitted, "*I'm* frustrated with me, so I know my kids are, too."

In their sessions, Melinda and Dr. Carter talked about her need to discern healthy anger from unhealthy anger. The doctor emphasized that she had choices in her anger management, so there was no question about her ability to change. She needed to remain focused on the better way. She looked forward to her sessions because she enjoyed the mental challenge.

In one of their discussions, Melinda was frank as she told Dr. Carter: "Something is not right inside of me. You and I have talked about the ways I can improve my handling of anger, and it all makes perfect sense as we discuss it in your office. When I get home, though, and I go two or three rounds with one of my kids, despite my good intentions, I'll blow up. In my mind, I can actually tell myself how to handle my anger correctly, and yet I'll let it come out wrong!"

Without consciously realizing it, Melinda would make the mistake of letting her emotional stability hinge almost entirely on the behavior of her children. As a Christian, she could have recited how she knew that God was her ultimate source of strength, but when push came to shove she would allow her kids to occupy the "God position" in her emotions. If they disobeyed persistently or if they argued too strongly, she became subconsciously convinced that she had no choice but to let her anger run.

Has this ever happened to you? When have you had good intentions to communicate anger correctly with your children, only to go in the wrong direction? (For instance, "Before we go out as a family I tell myself to be patient if my daughter is in a pouty mood, but when she whines I just lose it," or "I was shopping with my son for some clothes and he was so disagreeable that I was rude to him in front of the store clerk. I humiliated myself.")

_____

_____

_____

Many parents mistakenly assume that they can handle their anger correctly only after they get the children to respond to them properly. "Surely if my son sees that I'm trying to stay composed, he'll appreciate it and make a similar effort," the reasoning may go. If the child stays in an adversarial role, the parent reacts, "Just forget it! How am I supposed to stay on track if you're going to remain difficult?"

How do you sometimes allow your child to demotivate your desire to contain your emotions? (For instance, "My child has ADHD, and I get so flustered at his off-the-wall behavior," or "No matter how many times I talk to my daughter about it, she tells me lies; I wonder if there's something fundamentally wrong about my parenting methods.")

_____

_____

_____

Identifying Dependency

When your emotional responses are too easily tied to the behavior or responses of your child, you are displaying the trait of dependency. Many parents who are otherwise strong-willed, opinionated, or decisive may think, "Dependent? Me? I'm a highly independent person, so I don't think that trait describes me at all." Before dismissing the possibility that this quality is in play, let's get an idea of what it is. Dependency can be defined as allowing your mood or your inner direction to be determined by outer circumstances.

When Melinda allows her capacity for patience to hinge on Lexi's cooperative spirit, that is dependency at work. When she wants appreciation from Blake as they shop for clothes, but he can only grumble about it, her rudeness is a dependent response ("Because you won't act right, I won't either"). This is the thinking that dependency creates.

To get an idea of the role dependency plays in your relationship with your children, look over this list of reactions that are common to this trait. You may notice that other family members also have these qualities, so it could be enlightening for you to place the initials of the appropriate family member next to each item.

_____ Becoming edgy or frustrated when the other person says something you don't like
_____ Having a need to be accepted by others
_____ Losing sight of your good intentions once another person gives a wrong response
_____ Trying to force agreement when the other person disagrees
_____ Responding to griping with griping
_____ Becoming guarded when something unflattering is said about you
_____ Giving a reaction that is too strong for the circumstance
_____ Waiting for others to act as you wish before you can feel calm
_____ Working too hard to keep others in a good mood
_____ Being a reactor when you need to be an initiator

If you relate to at least five of these statements, it is an indication that your mood can be too tied to the situation in front of you. Your angry reaction may have a normal origin, but it may also be experienced more powerfully than necessary. You have to learn to allow your emotional direction to be less contingent on others' moods.

Is Dependency Wrong?

As Dr. Carter explained to Melinda that her anger could be driven by her dependency, she seemed somewhat alarmed. "Oh my!" she responded. "If dependency means that I'm too tied into my kids' reactions, then I guess I'll have to plead guilty. Lexi and Blake are constantly pulling my strings. I can start the day with a strong resolve not to get too angry about things, but after putting up with their erratic moods, I finally lose it."

"Don't assume that you're odd because of your reactions," the doctor assured her. "You're hardly experiencing anything different from most other parents. You're so emotionally invested in their well-being that it's normal for you to feel satisfied when you see how well they're doing, and it's just as normal to feel frustrated when they go astray."

Continuing in this vein, he further explained: "Even though the Bible does not mention dependency specifically, it's implied through the many 'one another' phrases. For instance, we're told to be kind to one another, to bear one another's burdens, to confess to one another, to encourage one another, and so on. Clearly our quality of life is enhanced when we can count on those closest to us to be considerate and thoughtful. God created us with a need for each other, and he knows that our quality of life is enhanced when we are coordinated in our key relationships. Rather than assuming that we should eliminate dependency, it's more reasonable to attempt to keep this characteristic in balance." This is a personal goal parents can aspire to, and they can also strive to help their kids achieve the same goal.

Your dependency has its origins in your own childhood. When you were born, you immediately cried out for someone to care for you, to give you nurturing. Once you were cleaned and wrapped in a blanket and cuddled, you calmed down. Every day afterward, you continued to display a similar hunger for attention and affection.

As the years passed, you looked to your own parents for love, encouragement, and support. When you felt confident that love and acceptance would be forthcoming, your mood was stable. Instinctively, you needed to hear regularly that the primary people in your life loved you and thought highly of you.

Did your dependency needs cease once you became a parent? Of course not. Though your sense of security ideally is stronger as an adult, you still want the primary people in your life (including your children) to display love and acceptance. This is normal.

What yearnings do you have toward your children that indicate you want their love and acceptance? (For example, "I hope that my daughter can appreciate the sacrifices I've made to help her do well in her extra-curricular activities," or "It would mean a lot to me if my son could express his love more openly.")

_____

_____

_____

If those yearnings are not satisfied, how are your emotions affected? (For instance, "When my daughter just seems selfish, it leaves me feeling used," or "When my son shuns my displays of affection, I feel hurt and disillusioned.")

_____

_____

_____

Just as you have dependency needs, so do your children. Because you are so primary to their emotional well-being, they look to you for assurance and nurturing. In each transaction with their parents, children entertain the questions, "Do I matter? Do you care about me? Can I count on you to understand me?"

As Melinda began examining why anger got out of hand in her home, she learned to focus on the role of dependency. For instance, she noted how Blake could be gregarious and charming with his teenage buddies, yet when she tried to talk about friction points with him he would clam up. "Being accepted by others is a big deal to Blake," she reflected to Dr. Carter. "There are times when he can be witty and funny and he knows that he can get virtually anyone to recognize that he's a delightful young man. As soon as problems surface, though, he goes into an emotional retreat. I think that the slightest potential for rejection causes him to mishandle anger altogether." Melinda was seeing the value of understanding the ingredients that lay at the root of her son's anger. Her insights would help her respond more constructively to his emotions.

"Lexi is much more open when she feels irritated, and it doesn't take much to set her off. She seems very easily hurt when I suggest that she's not doing something the way it ought to be done."

As you observe how your own children tend to respond according to the circumstances, how do you see their dependency at work? (For instance, "My son feels like he *has to* be with his friends, and when I ask him to stay at home he fears that his friends will be upset with him," or "My daughter is fine as long as everything goes her way, but once she has to adjust to someone else she can easily become moody.")

_____

_____

_____

Basically, when we are in an excessively dependent mode it means we are being reactors rather than initiators. We cease living according to our ideas of common sense, and we bend to the prevailing mood of the moment. Adding to this problem is the matter of codependency. *Co-* is a prefix meaning "with." Codependency is in play when two or more persons are so busy reacting to each other's moods that neither takes a healthy initiative. This pattern is extremely common in family relations as parents and children readily take their cues from each other, not pausing to discern what God would have them do in the circumstance.

When do you find yourself caught in a codependent pattern with your children? (For instance, "When my daughter sasses me, I can't hold back with a harsh rebuttal," or "When my son argues about my decisions, I'll go toe-to-toe with him.")

_____

_____

_____

Breaking the Codependent Pattern

As a leader that your children look to for guidance, you may not be able to immediately force them to act right, but you can certainly train yourself to opt out of the trap of codependency. To do so, you must determine separately from your children how you plan to manage your anger.

Think about some of your most common anger-provoking circumstances with your kids. What situations stand out most? (For instance, "Getting my daughter to get ready for school," or "Keeping my son from taunting his younger brother.")

_____

_____

_____

Think very carefully. What characteristics would you like to sustain as you respond to your child in those circumstances? (For instance, "I'd like to be more patient as I help my daughter prepare to leave the house each morning," or "I need to be calm and confident when my son is a troublemaker toward his brothers.")

_____

_____

_____

Too often, parents do not take the time to plan the traits they want to have in the face of an anger-provoking circumstance, making them susceptible to a spur-of-the-moment emotional response. In their sober moments, they can recite all sorts of instructions from the Bible that would prompt them to respond to life appropriately. For instance, most Christians are aware of biblical injunctions that tell us not to exchange insult for insult, or that we should contain the tongue (see I Peter 3:8–9 and James 3:5–10). Nonetheless, such knowledge remains stored away in the dark places of their minds as they are "helplessly" pulled along by the foul emotions of their children. Yet this need not be the case. It is possible to step out of your dependent mind-set to be the initiator of healthy traits. Your children may not respond to your initiative immediately, but you create improved conditions in your home as you (not the children) establish your own personal direction on the basis of what you know to be wise.

Recognizing how common dependency was proved to be a major breakthrough for Melinda. "I've always been a people person," she explained, "but I think that can get me into trouble when others display an unwillingness to make the relationship work. This is especially true when it comes to my children."

Breaking free from your codependent patterns will require an effort, yet it can be done. As you learn to identify the incidents in which a healthy initiative is needed, you realize that your dependent responses often are subconscious. By that we mean you do not consciously plan to let your mood be dictated by your child; it happens without your being aware of the tendency. Once you become conscious of the situations in which you become dependent, and as you become aware of the better choices you can make at those times, you are well on your way to breaking your anger cycle.

Competence in Emotions

To break out of your dependency, you need to view yourself as emotionally competent. That is, you are not destined to merely allow your mood to be set by your children. Despite their many emotional highs and lows, you can determine to chart your own healthy course during frustrating circumstances.

We firmly hold the belief that each individual possesses a God-given competence to have stable emotions, even when the environment is not friendly. To think otherwise leads to utter defeat. Even if you have not applied your competence consistently, be assured that you have it.

When you were a child, you needed your own parents to guide you carefully through your emotional choices. For instance, whenever you felt angry toward a sibling, a parent might take the time to walk you through your options regarding communication of that anger. Likewise, if you felt intimidated by an overpowering person, a parent might discuss your feelings regarding your circumstances and you would learn that you could choose the direction to take in response to that situation.

When you were a youngster, how were emotionally charged circumstances addressed? (For instance, "My dad just barked out orders and I tried to comply," or "My mother stayed so tense, she really couldn't talk with me about how I felt.")

_____

_____

_____

The message to be sent to you early in life was that you were indeed capable of sifting through your choices even when your world was unfriendly or uncooperative. If you did not receive training to ferret out your emotional options, it does not mean you are incompetent to do so. It only means that you were not trained at the ideal time in your life. You can still discover your own competence today.

Melinda shook her head as she discussed this matter with Dr. Carter. "I don't think my parents ever considered the possibility of discussing my emotional responses with me. They divorced when I was eleven, which means that they had their own issues to work out. My mother, in particular, was so overwhelmed with her problems that she barely had the energy to talk with me about my own struggles."

"Melinda, it would have been ideal if your folks had capitalized on the opportunities to map out your emotional responses with you. The fact that they didn't is frustrating because it meant that you remained in your reactor mode when you could have taken a more self-motivated path. The good news, though, is that you still have the competence to make separate choices regarding your emotional direction. You'll have to consciously choose not to indulge some of the lightning-quick responses that plague you when anger comes upon you. Yet better options are certainly at your disposal."

"I hope you're right," came her reply. "My pessimism can sometimes get the best of me because I feel so frustrated by my children when they absolutely refuse to respect me."

Dr. Carter continued: "There's one word that you need to sidestep as you make plans to break your dependency upon your children. It's the word _can't_. When you tell yourself that you can't deal with them or that you can't come up with a mature response, you are conceding defeat before you even begin."

When are you most inclined to tell yourself that you can't manage a situation in your home? (For instance, "When my son goes around my back and aligns my husband against me," or "When my kids won't stop arguing no matter how strongly I apply consequences.")

_____

_____

_____

In those moments when it seems tempting to collapse under the weight of *can't*, you have to be extra attentive to the reality of your competence. You may feel like letting your anger run away with you, but it is still possible to make wise choices. You must make room for the reality that the people in your presence are not making wise emotional choices, but that does not require you to join them.

As you choose to think of yourself as competent to make wise decisions in frustrating circumstances, your chances of success increase as you have a greater sense of purpose guiding you. Rather than haphazardly responding to each situation as best as you can, your choices can be a part of a well-conceived mission.

Dr. Carter asked Melinda what her mission was as a parent. She stammered a bit as she tried to give an intelligent reply. "Well, I guess it's my job to see that my kids grow up with good values and that they learn to treat people as they wish to be treated. Is that the kind of answer you're looking for?" Clearly, she was caught off guard by the question.

"Yes, that sounds like a good enough answer," came the reply, "but I want you to think less about giving me the correct answer and focus more on what truly drives you."

"Well to be honest, that's not the kind of question I think about very often. I guess if you really pressed me I could come up with a more complete answer regarding my mission as a parent, but honestly it would probably seem like an academic exercise rather than something that's truly from the heart."

Staying with the theme of competence, Dr. Carter explained: "Your responses of anger toward your children will always be erratic if you're not consciously aware of how those responses fit into the larger picture. Rather than letting the immediate circumstance determine your emotions, you can learn to be guided by a much greater cause."

How about you? What would you say is your mission as a parent? (For instance, "I want my son to be filled with confidence and consideration of others, and I want him to be comfortable dealing with the personal dimensions of life," or "I want my daughter to know how to apply our spiritual beliefs in a manner that shows her to be a caring and respectful person.")

_____

_____

_____

What causes you to lose sight of that mission? (For instance, "Often my anger gets out of bounds because I'm so time-focused that my only thought is to get my daughter to do things when they're supposed to be done," or "Honestly, I'm not the kind of person to think much about philosophical things like my mission as a parent.")

_____

_____

_____

How can your anger responses improve if you specifically focus on your parental mission? (For instance, "I'd respond to my child, knowing that our every contact has meaning," or "I'd be less impulsive and more deliberate in the way I confront.")

_____

_____

_____

Dr. Carter spoke with Melinda: "You've probably heard someone say something to the effect that you only have one chance at life, so make the most of it. It's that kind of thinking that I hope will guide you in your dealings with Blake and Lexi."

Reflecting out loud, Melinda interjected: "I know that what you're saying is true. I guess I can get so caught up in the mood of the moment that my deeper beliefs are left somewhere else. I can honestly say that it's been too long since I've truly taken the time to ponder where I'm trying to go with my anger. The immediate frustration causes me to lose sight of my good parenting goals."

Proverbs 22:6 gives the familiar instruction to "train up a child in the way he should go and when he is old he will not depart from it." It certainly would have been ideal if your own parents had spent many moments going over your strategies for handling emotions and relational problems. Even in the absence of such training, your adult life is not hopeless. You can still determine how to proceed in trying circumstances, and as you do you can also determine to give your children the guidance you may not have received in your earlier years.

As your kids grow older—certainly by the preteen and teenage years—it can be helpful for the entire family to discuss your collective mission. Your children need to hear from you regarding the beliefs that drive your behaviors and emotions. They need to be challenged by you to grapple with their own building sense of purpose. As you repeatedly discuss the initiatives you each can take in a moment of conflict, a team spirit develops and you manage anger with a positive purpose.

In one session, Melinda told Dr. Carter about a discussion she had with Blake and Lexi. "I explained to them that I was under the conviction that I had been responding to conflict with little forethought about where it was leading. I told them that my goal was to stay grounded in respectfulness even as I talked with them about my frustrations. I even gave them an example of how I intended to moderate my voice the next time I caught them bickering."

"How did they respond to that kind of talk?"

"Well, they weren't real sure how to take it at first. You have to understand that it hasn't been our practice to go into philosophical discussions. Once I told them about my mission, I then challenged each of them to do the same. I asked them to think carefully about the qualities they'd like to guide their lives. Then I mentioned that the real test would come during our moments of conflict. I explained that we need to realize that we just can't go on being reactors, with no game plan guiding us. Then we discussed options they had regarding some of the common problems that triggered angry responses." The doctor smiled as he realized that she was a living example of Proverbs 22:6.

Are you willing to lead your children in some discussions about your family's purpose and how it can be applied in conflict? How do you think your kids will respond? (For instance, "My son would probably think it is dumb to talk about personal things," or "My daughter seems to like it when we have more adult-like conversations.")

_____

_____

_____

You probably will not succeed in immediately changing the codependent patterns of managing anger, but with ongoing attention to higher plans you can slowly get away from being a sheer reactor.

Small Increments of Time

As Dr. Carter talked with Melinda about breaking dependency's hold on her anger responses, he cautioned her about expecting perfect results: "It's well and good to plan to let traits like calmness and respectfulness lead the way in your anger-provoking circumstances, but it's not always natural. Many times you'll find yourself going back into the old reactions that you don't like."

"Actually, I'm glad to hear you say that," Melinda said, "because I know myself well enough to know that I'll be inconsistent. Usually, I'll wallow in guilt and frustration as I scold myself for failing one more time."

"If it makes you feel any better, I'm not perfect either as a parent," he replied. "I have found one technique, though, that helps to keep me on track when I notice my bad moods are about to take over. That is, I can give myself brief and focused assignments about my immediate use of anger."

Let's say, for instance, that you have determined to be patient rather than brash in a moment of anger. This is certainly a noble goal, and it can help you remain within your overall mission as a parent. Honesty requires you, though, to admit that you cannot expect to be patient in every situation for the rest of your life. You can, however, determine to allow patience to be part of your response for the next thirty minutes! Rather than telling yourself that forevermore you must be a patient parent, you can plan how patience will play out in the next half hour.

For instance, Melinda was able to target seven-thirty to eight o'clock each school morning as a time when she would be most vulnerable to anger. Her dependency could be so strong that she would allow her mood to be determined by Lexi's level of cooperation in getting ready for school. Given the girl's track record of sluggishness, it would not be wise for Melinda to look to her to set up a good mood. Melinda therefore learned to talk specifically to herself regarding her mission as a parent during the time from seven-thirty to eight o'clock. "I want to be firm, yet I also want to be respectful," she would say to herself. So she accepted the challenge that from seven-thirty to eight o'clock, no matter how disrespectful Lexi acted, she would remain firm but respectful. At one minute past eight, she might decide to explode, but from seven-thirty to eight o'clock she would remain fixed on her own initiative.

Can you learn to think about being an initiator of a good response in small increments of time? What are some of the common times or circumstances when you can choose to be an initiator instead of a reactor? (For instance, "The first hour when my girls come home from school sets the pace for the rest of the evening. I could choose patience between four o'clock and five o'clock today," or "When my son tells me his plans to be with other boys that are a bad influence on him, I can determine that during those specific interchanges, I'll remain calm and firm.")

_____

_____

_____

Dependency will always be a trait in your personality, and it will always come into play as you determine how to respond to your children when they are disagreeable. You will never want to become so disconnected from them that you cease to react to them at all. That would imply apathy. Yet you can choose to have a separate-enough plan for your own emotional responses that you can rise above their immature responses and be the leader you need to be.

The psalmist was certainly one who loved to be challenged with God's thoughts as he considered how to conduct his life. "Oh how I love your law," he wrote. "It is my meditation all the day. You, through your commandments, make me wiser than my enemies; for they are ever with me" (Psalm 119:97–98). He understood fully the folly of letting events dictate his direction each day, given the fickle nature of people and circumstances. Parents can find similar solace as they take time regularly to contemplate who God wants them to be and how his instructions are relevant to the many situations in the home. This requires time out to think, pray, and listen to God's leading. It is a certainty that such proactive planning for life skills will prove superior to haphazardly letting your mood be dictated by your children's moodiness.

To keep balance in your responses of dependency, let go of the need to be in control of them. We discuss this matter in the next chapter.

For Family Discussion

1. Codependency happens when individuals feed on one another's foul moods and circumstances go from bad to worse. Have each family member describe two or three times when they have been pulled in by another person's bad mood.

2. Have each person list eight or nine traits that you wish could be most prominent in your personality. Then share your lists out loud. This is a beginning effort in defining who you want to be.

3. Now, share with each other when you are least likely to live with the traits you have listed. What does this reveal about your tendency to depend on others to set your mood?

4. Have each person write a mission statement for his or her role within the family; then let each person read it out loud. Ask each person to answer the question, "How does your use of anger fit into the mission statement?"

5. When we state that each person has competence to choose their own direction in anger management, we mean that each person is capable of making responsible choices. Have each person identify two or three common incidents when you could take greater responsibility for your emotional choices.

6. When your dependency is balanced, you seek less control over outer circumstances because you are more concerned with your own inner direction. Have the family members describe how they would benefit by concentrating more on their own choices and less on others' actions.

For Further Reflection

Romans 12:10 instructs that Christians should be devoted to one another, while verse 12:16 instructs us to be of the same mind toward one another.

1. What are some additional common "one another" instructions found in the Bible? How can these "one another" behaviors be applied to the parent-child relationship?

2. How can you determine when family members are so affected by one another that it undermines the ability to manage anger successfully? What signs indicate that your mood is too easily affected by your children, or that their mood is too tied to you?

The apostle Paul stated in Philippians 4:11: "I have learned to be content in whatever circumstances I am."

3. How might your children rob you of the ability to be consistently content? How might your use of anger disrupt your children's ability to find contentment from God?

4. Ideally, how should a content parent handle frustrations and anger caused by disruptive children?

Psalm 8:5 indicates that each person is "crowned with glory and majesty."

5. How is your communication of anger affected as you remember that your children represent the handiwork of God's creative genius? How can your use of anger remain consistent with the notion that your children are of the highest value to you and to God?

6. What qualities would you expect to see in parents whose moods are not dependent upon their children's reactions? In what circumstances do you need to concentrate most keenly on the purpose of teaching your children about their God-given worth?

5

DROPPING EXCESSIVE CONTROL

STEP 5: Realize that the best way to be in control is to diminish control tactics, speaking instead about choices.

Discipline. Structure. Accountability. These are key values that parents rightly want to instill in their children. If your kids are to succeed in their later adult pursuits, they have to learn the value of reliability during their childhood years. As a result, it becomes the parents' job to teach respect for harmony and responsibility from the earliest years onward.

That said, there is no guarantee that children will appreciate their parents' efforts to teach principles of cooperation and thoughtfulness. For instance, you may instruct your son to take responsibility for cleaning his room, yet he may immediately conclude that you are totally insensitive for making such a request. Or perhaps you have talked many times with your daughter about the need to associate with the right people, and she persistently ignores your instructions. Has anything of this nature ever happened in your home?

Commonly, when parents communicate their desires to their children, the interaction quickly produces a power struggle as the child prefers one option while the parent prefers another. A battle for control ensues as each becomes stubborn, forceful, or belligerent. At the heart of this battle is the emotion of anger. Have you determined how you can respond to this struggle for control with the least amount of misapplied anger?

One of the most difficult challenges for Christians is to know when and how to stand firmly for right principles while at the same time allowing others the space to decipher for themselves who they will be. We Christians can be quite grounded in matters of right and wrong because, after all, we have the authority of the Bible telling us the proper way to live. As we attempt to stand firmly upon our values and convictions, particularly as parents, we can be so zealous in our efforts that we forget that God has entrusted each person—including children—with free will. The parent's need for correctness often clashes directly with a child's need to feel free, and the net result is angry conflict.

Ron was the father of three sons, ages fifteen, twelve, and nine; and a seven-year-old daughter. He grew up in a home where his own dad seemed to communicate only when he was scolding or ordering Ron to act exactly as he prescribed. Other than that, it seemed as if his father excused himself from the nurturing part of parenting. When Ron became a father, he vowed that he would be attentive to his kids' personal needs, both in the fun times and in the moments when quiet teaching was needed. Now, fifteen years deep into his paternal role, he could very proudly state that he was indeed the hands-on dad that his father had not been toward him.

Ron's kids would readily attest to his active participation in many aspects of their lives, but they would also indicate that it came with a painful emotional price. Ron certainly had moments of congeniality, but he could also speak to his children in abrupt, commanding tones. Predictably, his children did not like it when he became overbearing, and increasingly the home experienced tension and discord as the struggle for control ensued.

As an illustration, the fifteen-year-old, Ethan, was a happy-go-lucky socialite who lived for the next opportunity to be with his friends. With many connections at school and in his church youth group, he never lacked for things to do. His problem was that he would gladly put off school assignments to give priority to his social life. His grades were slipping, and Ron learned that he would often tell lies to cover his irresponsibility.

Put yourself in Ron's shoes. Each time he emphasized the need for Ethan to complete his school work first before pursuing other activities, his son would smile and assure him that he would do so. Yet Ron would frequently uncover Ethan's irresponsibility and insist that he follow through on his promises. After many disappointing episodes with his son, do you suppose that it was reasonable or normal for Ron to feel angry?

You have probably been where Ron was many times with your own children. You can be quite clear in communicating your messages to your kids, but they buck you, disobey, give a half-hearted effort, or grumble. Like Ron, you feel angry, and the emotion is quite normal and understandable.

In what circumstances does your communication with your children turn into a contest of will? (For instance, "When I tell my daughter to turn off the TV, almost always she responds with a plea to keep watching," or "When I discuss curfew times with my son, he predictably complains about how unreasonable it is to have a curfew.")

When your discipline efforts are met with resistance, how are you affected emotionally? (For instance, "I become very weary when my daughter talks back, and it makes me feel edgy," or "Irritability and impatience quickly come over me when I have to listen to my son griping about the family rules.")

As anger builds inside during these moments, what is *right* about your emotions? (For instance, "It is right for me to want basic cooperation at home," or "It is right to think that my child should respect my position of authority.")

_____

_____

_____

Once your anger is pricked during such a struggle, it is easy for your anger to intensify as you yearn to have control. The more you try to control, the greater the tension between yourself and your child. In the short run, you may be able to force your child to do things your way, but as the years pass and you persist in controlling measures, your influence can drop sharply.

To get an idea of your inclination toward controlling responses, look over this list of traits common to control. Check the ones that apply to you fairly frequently.

_____ Speaking in commands or strong directives
_____ Interrupting for the purpose of getting your point across
_____ Using a sharp or harsh tone of voice
_____ Speaking in threats and making intimidating statements
_____ Pleading and using persuasive language, often in question form ("Why won't you cooperate?" or "What's gotten into you?")
_____ Becoming impatient when others are not cooperative
_____ Stubbornly refusing to acknowledge the legitimacy of the other person's perspective
_____ Being so correct that the ability to be loving is temporarily displaced
_____ Responding to mistakes or flaws with agitation
_____ Becoming caught in an exchange of rebuttals
_____ Being repetitious when expressing something of importance
_____ Maintaining a glaring look or having an uninviting appearance
_____ Being unbending in your opinions and preferences

We each have moments when we fall into controlling communication, so it would be abnormal if you did not relate to any of these traits. If you do check at least five of these qualities, it is probable that your need for control pushes your anger beyond constructive boundaries. You undoubtedly create more problems in your anger than you solve.

What controlling behavior would you say is most common in yourself? (For instance, "I will out-argue my son when he talks back," or "I tend to speak in an unwavering, authoritarian manner when I'm getting my point across.")

_____

_____

_____

What's So Bad About Control?

Ron sought counseling with Dr. Carter because he realized his anger was increasingly frequent and intense. As they got to know each other, Dr. Carter eventually focused on Ron's tendency to be heavy-handed in trying to control his children's responses. Frequently, Ron would issue a challenging statement to them: "I'd better not hear one more word of back-talk from you." Sometimes he would ask questions that were meant to intimidate: "What am I going to have to do to get you to understand that I mean business?" Other times he would erupt with forcefulness: "All right, that does it! I'm fed up with your attitude and you're going to be sorry for making trouble around here." With each response, Ron raised his voice considerably and ugly arguments would commonly follow.

Speaking to this issue, the doctor said, "Ron, I'm learning that in your anger toward your children you go readily into the control mode. Forcefulness seems to be a common trait that you fall back on."

"Well, it's true," he responded. "I can't just let my kids think they can get away with all sorts of irresponsible behavior. Sometimes my kids can be incredibly stubborn, and they need constant reminders that I won't tolerate their bad attitude. Are you suggesting that I should just go easy on them and let them get away with mayhem?"

"Not at all. Children's minds are not so fully developed that they can be expected to know how to harmonize their every need with the needs of others. They must have adults to teach them that there are certain parameters to consider in daily lifestyle choices. What I am suggesting is that you examine how controlling you sound as you communicate your good ideas to them. When you overdo the coercion, your influence eventually decreases to nothing."

Control within a family is necessary, to the extent that courtesy and responsibility are taught as the desirable way to live. Structure is a necessary part of society, so it is good for children to respect structure at home. Because most kids learn to be responsible only after they are taught to do so, firmness and accountability are qualities that parents need as they play the role of teacher. Yet even as parents exert control in their home, they must be mindful that overuse of control can have disastrous results.

One of the primary problems that has plagued human nature since the disaster in the garden of Eden is the struggle for control. God told Adam and Eve not to eat of the Tree of Knowledge of Good and Evil, yet they did. This was the first instance of humans exerting a controlling spirit, and it set into motion a determination to go one's own way even if it meant defying God. Ever since that day, each human has had problems discerning control boundaries. Just as Adam and Eve succumbed to the temptation to "be like God" (see Genesis 3:5), each of us can be seduced to act in a Godlike manner toward those in our lives. Parents today need to maintain a system of controls with their children, of course; but they must also commit to balance as they determine not to let their control tendencies become too forceful or pushy.

As an example, Ron's twelve-year-old, Chase, was well on his way to major problems, and much of it was driven by his reactions to strong control. "He's only in the seventh grade," Ron explained to the doctor, "but I think he may already be experimenting with some very dangerous behavior. One of his friends who's a couple of years older was arrested for distributing marijuana. Chase says he's never smoked it, but I don't really believe him. He seems to be attracted to peers who openly disregard authority, and he sure has a bad attitude at home. He doesn't argue a lot, like Ethan does. He just won't do what he's told. He stays withdrawn in his room, and sometimes it takes dynamite to get him motivated to do anything we ask. The more I lean on him to do right, the more he sulks and pouts."

Has anything like this ever happened in your home? What kind of resistance do you encounter when you try to force your children to comply? (For instance, "When I grounded my daughter because she and a friend openly defied my rules, my daughter barely spoke to me for a week," or "I caught my son going where he wasn't supposed to go, and when I called him on it he somehow rationalized that it was my fault.")

_____

_____

_____

Children know they need structure and order. Nevertheless, they can sometimes challenge parents so strongly that the parents need to illustrate that they, not the child, are still the ones who set the rules. How this is accomplished is crucial. Does your communication take on a condescending spirit, or are you able to remain firm even as you are also consistent with loving motives?

Be an Authority, Not Authoritarian

Remember that clean, assertive anger is displayed when you preserve your convictions while also demonstrating respect toward the one you are angry with. When parents find their children in a pattern of chronic disrespect toward authority, it is often due to the parents' overuse of that authority. Too many parents display their power in a manner that leaves the child feeling greatly disrespected, but they seem genuinely perplexed that the child would respond poorly.

When taking the authoritarian role, parents do best to remember that leadership is established as loving traits are prominent. When leaders act like dictators (whether in a government, a business, or a home) their subordinates may comply in fear, but ultimately those subordinates look for an escape hatch. Christ's leadership style was anchored not in an iron-fisted manner but in love, flexibility, and fair-mindedness. He could certainly speak firmly when necessary, but his overall tone was noncoercive.

Ron recounted how twelve-year-old Chase had been displaying growing rebellion for two years or so. "It seems like he's appointed himself as his own final authority," Ron said, "but I am absolutely determined to remind him that he is definitely not in charge of this household." Ron went on to explain that he had butted heads numerous times in recent months with Chase, and he was not going to slow down until his son learned to comply.

"Ron, your desire for structure at home is very reasonable. But I'm concerned that in cracking down on Chase, you seem to be losing him." They discussed how Chase's reactions of rebellion could actually be understood as an attempt to prove that he was not as powerless as his dad seemed to want him to be. The doctor went on to explain: "When a youngster at that age feels he is up against a dictatorial regime, he loses hope and decides that he might as well do what he wants to do. If parents are so authoritarian that they leave little room for choice, their kids react like a dog locked inside a fence. As soon as the dog sees an opening, it bolts!"

What signs do you see in your children that they are weary of heavy authority? (For instance, "My daughter has gotten into a habit of not looking at me or rolling her eyes when we talk about discipline matters," or "My son openly defies what I tell him to do.")

_____

_____

_____

To offset your child's poor response to your efforts to maintain control, there are three key ingredients that can help you keep the relationship whole: (1) Say yes as often as common sense allows, (2) use consequences as a means to back up your words, and (3) emphasize choice over obligation.

Be a *Yes* Person When Common Sense Allows It

Think back to your own childhood and teen years. As each year passed, more and more adventures opened to you. If you were like most, you wanted to participate in activities with peers. You definitely did not want to be known as the kid whose parents wouldn't let you do the things that your social group did. You wanted to feel free to grow, expand, and try on new things.

Your children are no different. They want to fit in with their peers. They want to participate in fun activities. They want to comb their hair differently or wear clothes that are not exactly what you would pick out. They may act silly or feel emotions that you do not. Are you willing to allow them to have their own unique preferences? We are not suggesting that you have no standards or rules, only that you accept that your children are not always going to be the same as you . . . and that can be good.

Speculate for a moment about how your children see you. Do they see you as a *yes* person or a *no* person? Explain. (For instance, "My son seems hesitant when he asks about going out with his friends, as if he expects me to be negative," or "I've had moments when I've squashed my daughter's enthusiasm because I'm too busy pointing out the potential problems.")

_____

_____

_____

The more your children think of you as a *no* person, the more they feel confined or controlled. In their earlier years, you might be able to succeed in forcing your will upon them, but as they age they learn to be devious to get out from under your regulations.

That was the problem Ron was having with both Ethan and Chase. Ethan had pointedly told him, "Dad, there's no sense in me asking you if I can do something because it's a guarantee that you'll say no. You want things exactly your way, and you can't stand it if I have different ideas."

Dr. Carter explained to Ron, "God has given each person free will. Very young children are too immature to make wise free choices, so parents need to step in often with specific directions. As the kids grow older, they still need your guidance but are naturally going to want a say in the things that happen to them. In other words, they want to use their God-given free will. They will only incorporate your input willingly if they sense that you're for them, not against them. Right now, to change the atmosphere at home, they have to know that you actually want them to learn how to make free choices. If they only hear *no*, you will lose credibility. They want to know that you respect the fact they can begin to think for themselves."

How do your children act out their frustration when they sense there is too much of a *no* mentality at home? (For instance, "My daughter pouts and fumes for hours," or "My son is very argumentative and constantly challenges my authority.")

_____

_____

_____

How will your relationship with your children improve if you are more willing to say yes? Where should you start? (For instance, "I can be more flexible in letting my son decide how and when he'll take care of school assignments," or "I need to listen more to my daughter's feelings about her social involvements.")

_____

_____

_____

Certainly there are times when parents have to act with discernment, as they plan with their children how to address their needs as they relate to the greater needs of the family. In most cases, though, your children feel more affirmed and less controlled if you take the time to elicit their opinions and make an effort to accommodate their legitimate desires. As you maintain a reputation of encouragement and fair-mindedness, the possibilities of diminishing the anger at home increase.

Use Consequences Wisely

Virtually every parenting manual emphasizes the need for children to understand that each free choice is followed by consequences. In general, parents can communicate to the child that a cooperative spirit brings the consequences of positive privileges, while a combative spirit incurs loss of privileges. Most parents already implement some system of consequences, even if it is not always well conceived.

For your anger level to remain balanced, your methods of communicating consequences must be temperate. Too often we find that parents create a greater possibility for tension because they communicate consequences threateningly or coercively as opposed to speaking about consequences with calm firmness. We have already mentioned how Ephesians 6:4 instructs fathers not to provoke their children to anger. We take this to mean that the method of communicating is of equal importance to the actual words that are communicated (if not even greater in importance). Forceful words may have an element of correctness, but the intended message can be completely lost if respect is not registered. Consequences must be spoken, then, not as a threat but in a plain, matter-of-fact tone of voice.

Ron told Dr. Carter about an exchange between himself and Chase that typified the controlling manner that so commonly fueled his anger. Chase went out with some older boys that Ron had identified as trouble-makers. Chase let his father assume that he would be going out with a friend who was clean-cut, but instead he went to the house of an older boy who introduced him to his father's liquor cabinet. When Ron learned that his son had deceived him and been drinking, he hit the roof: "Let me tell you a thing or two, young man. You can lie out of your teeth if that's what you want to do and you can get drunk with those bums if you think that's so fun, but when I catch you, there's going to be hell to pay! I'll ground you so long that you'll never see daylight again. What do you think about that?" His voice was harsh and loud.

Clearly Ron's anger had a reasonable purpose, and clearly this was a situation that required a consequence. Even so, the method of communicating the anger had such a controlling and abrasive edge that the reasonableness of his message was almost certain to be lost. You can imagine how Chase received his father's words.

When have you had legitimate times to apply consequences that were communicated in a way that made the message hard for your child to digest? (For instance, "When my daughter recently lied to me about her weekend activities, I was very condescending as I told her how she would be punished," or "When I try to break up my children from their bickering, I tend to give exaggerated consequences because at the moment I'm so angry.")

_____

_____

_____

_____

Even though your anger may be motivated by a right conviction, if the method of communicating is overpowering or rigid the child is inclined to react to the tension of the emotion and does not grasp the correctness of the message. Children need to learn that their choices have consequences, so to set the stage for that learning to occur it has to be presented logically, as opposed to being presented with heavy persuasion.

Dr. Carter coached Ron how he might have handled his anger in a less controlling manner even while teaching Chase that his poor decisions would have consequences. "The first thing you'll need to do," he explained, "is to pull away from the temptation to speak coercively. Your tone of voice has to be even, not commanding. It would be very reasonable to tell Chase that you're disappointed that he deceived you about who he was with. It would also be reasonable to let him know that you strongly disapprove of his using alcohol. Chase is probably expecting some form of discipline, so you can clearly let him know that a consequence will be applied. All the while, you'll need to keep a calm, yet firm, tone of voice."

"I know that yelling doesn't help matters any, but I'm not sure I can do the calm part."

Dr. Carter reminded him: "Yelling at him will always remain an option, but I'm hoping you've learned by now that it almost never works. The purpose of expressing anger is ultimately to address the issues that are hindering love. You love your son and you don't want to see him taking a totally wrong path at this delicate age. He needs to know that's why you feel upset. It's reasonable to ground him for what he did or to remove favorite privileges. As you remove the control from your voice and let your resolve be accompanied by concern, he is more likely to re-ceive what you have to say in the spirit of love."

Certainly you will have times when you must apply consequences to your child's poor choices. How can you address this matter with a non-coercive spirit? (For instance, "I need to just say what the consequences will be, as opposed to piling on the guilt," or "Too often I display my anger as a means of showing my kids who's in charge, and they don't see that it's my love that compels me to apply consequences.")

_____

_____

_____

There are several adjustments that can help you communicate about consequences, but with a minimum of controlling anger:

_____ Remove coercion and persuasion from your tone of voice. Let your words be spoken with firm resolve.

_____ Stay away from questions that are not meant to gather infor-mation (such as "What's wrong with you?" or "What did we talk about just yesterday?").

_____ Avoid putting your child on a guilt trip. Shaming kids is a poor motivator.

_____ Discuss openly the better alternatives to the behaviors or attitudes in question. Get the child to talk about other options that can be explored.

_____ Involve the child in deciding what the consequences might be.

_____ Explain why you are applying consequences, but don't go into a heavy defense of your decisions when the child questions your reasoning.

When you work too hard to convince your child of the validity of your thoughts, the child can interpret it as an invitation to argue. As you decrease your persuasion, your message has a greater chance of getting through to the child.

Emphasize Choice over Obligation

As you emphasize control less, you recognize the value of choices. Think ahead to how life will be for your children once they are old enough to leave home and face the world of adult responsibilities. They will have wide-open freedom, meaning they will be privileged to choose for themselves how they will handle life. In the years prior to that full freedom, they need plenty of practice in sifting through the many issues requiring wise decision making. If parents go overboard in controlling how their children should think or act, they leave them ill-prepared for the adult years.

The Old Testament leader Joshua was frustrated as he recognized that the people of his country were turning away from God and toward paganism. He spoke openly but noncoercively with them about this problem as he explained: "Choose for yourselves today whom you will serve . . . but as for me and my house, we will serve the Lord." He did not say "I command you to do what is right" because that would not have been enforceable. He exemplified the same mind-set that parents today can use with their children: put the choices in front of them, and then give them room to decide.

What essential issues do you foresee your children having to tackle once they are old enough to leave home? (For instance, "They will need to know how to budget money wisely," or "They will need to have good strategies for managing conflict.")

_____

_____

_____

If your communication with your children consists of little more than telling them what to do or how to think, you deprive them of the skills needed to gain ownership of their beliefs and priorities. Though it may require some patience along the way, you do them a favor by letting them have room to grapple with their current problems.

Dr. Carter worked with Ron to shift his emphasis when he was in conflict with Ethan and Chase. They strategized how he could switch controlling responses to a communication style that emphasized choices: "When you're feeling angry with your sons, I'm assuming that your anger is pushed along by a desire to teach your boys good values. Being belligerent or overbearing hinders you from getting your right message across. Instead, you might try urging them to examine the choices they have in the circumstance that is under question."

When Chase taunts his younger brother and sister regarding petty matters, for instance, instead of just yelling at him for his wrong behavior Ron can discuss choices with him: "If your sister is bothering you by coming into your room, taunting her is an option, but it's not a good one. Let's take the time to explore what your better options are."

Here are some other examples of positive ways to express anger:

_____ If Chase continues to hold onto his abrasive attitude, Ron might say, "You can continue being argumentative. That's an option, but keep in mind that it comes with the consequence of no TV or computer for the rest of the day. You could also choose to have a cooperative spirit, and that would bring you the consequence of full privileges. Which do you choose?"

_____ If Ethan is going out on Friday night to a ballgame with his friends, instead of issuing a hard curfew time Ron can talk with him on a more mature level: "Let's get an idea of what sorts of things you'll be doing this evening so you and I can determine a reasonable time for you to come in."

_____ If Ethan disrespects the time parameters that they decide on, Ron can still speak with respect to choices: "Ethan, I see that you choose to go counter to our time frame, so let's talk about the consequences and how we should proceed from here."

There are numerous ways your children can disobey you or act annoyingly. In these incidents your anger can certainly be aroused, and that anger is often linked to a message that the child *needs* to hear. You can choose to speak in a controlling manner and force compliance; it will probably only embitter the child, but nonetheless that is one of your options. You can also choose to address the anger-provoking circumstance with a discussion about options and consequences. To do so, apply self-restraint and think more creatively as you express yourself. If you take this route, you will have a better chance of succeeding in getting the message of your anger across to the child.

In what circumstances can you choose to discuss your child's options, as opposed to being controlling with your anger? (For instance, "When my daughter gripes about my requirements for cooperation with her siblings, we can discuss options regarding what would be wise to say at that moment," or "When my son challenges me after I've said it's time for his friends to leave, we could later discuss his ideas about the appropriate ways to handle his disappointment.")

_____

_____

_____

If you repeatedly say to your children, "Let's discuss your options," they will eventually come to expect you to talk with them in that fashion. Though they may not immediately like going through this type of introspection, you are sending the message that you want them to learn to think for themselves, as opposed to your doing the thinking on their behalf.

Control Is an Illusion

We have spoken with many parents who persist in their anger because they are unwilling to lay down their need to be in control. We remind them that they can continue to choose to use force and coercion with their children, but if they do so they should be prepared for their kids to respond with foul anger, and that they (the parents) will experience greater intensity in their own anger.

To be willing to let go of controlling attitudes, you have to embrace a core truth: control is an illusion. In the short run, parents may be able to control their children through coercion, but as the years pass the children will actively look for ways to express themselves freely. That self-expression often comes in the form of misbehavior or defiance if there has been insufficient freedom to express themselves openly or to choose how to handle their own circumstances.

Ron had mixed reactions each time he and Dr. Carter spoke about dropping his controlling ways so as to communicate with a greater perspective of freedom. "On the one hand, I can remember how I didn't want my own parents telling me what to do when I was young," he would say. "I can distinctly recall feeling belittled when my dad wouldn't let me have any input regarding decisions involving my life." Then showing his perplexity, he admitted, "I just feel really shaky sometimes when I talk to my kids about choices. It feels as if I'm being weak."

The doctor was sympathetic. "Sure enough, you're taking a risk in being less controlling and more willing to allow a broader array of emotional expressions and behavioral choices. My hope is, though, that as you give your kids plenty of practice in sifting through their choices now, when they're nineteen and on their own they'll be more skilled in making wise decisions because of your willingness to talk about choices at this earlier stage in their development."

In what way do you feel shaky when you talk with your children about choices? (For instance, "My daughter is so boy-crazy that I'm afraid she won't display good boundaries in her social life," or "I honestly cannot tolerate some of my son's taste in music or television or movies.")

_____

_____

_____

Keep in mind that your willingness to be less controlling does not have to translate into having no standards. You can still be very clear about your values, and when necessary you can still apply consequences if your children go too far out of bounds. Our aim is not to have you surrender your convictions, but to communicate them with the realization that you cannot force your children to think exactly as you do.

Be aware that along with your spoken communication, your children are reading between the lines and interpreting your feelings on a different, more covert level. For instance, when you communicate your anger in a controlling manner, your unspoken message is one of no trust. They feel belittled. This is why controlling parents tend to lose influence with each passing year. If you ease up on the controls and speak your anger in an even tone of voice, appealing to choices, your influence increases. They feel as if you have a measure of faith in their abilities.

Ultimately, when you favor choices over coercion, you lay the groundwork for your children to understand the nature of grace, which is the gift of love that is unattached to performance. As Christians, we can approach God with the understanding that we are not obliged to act perfectly according to his Law; we are free to be imperfect humans. God still speaks to us through Scripture about the correct way to live, and we still experience consequences when we choose to live outside his truth. If we realize that his grace will cause him to relate lovingly with us despite our flaws, though, the choice to obey him becomes easier. Love, not forcefulness, is what enables the mind to assimilate truth.

Assuming you can learn to be honest about your anger, yet do so gracefully, what positive impact might this have on your relationship with your children? (For instance, "We would have a much less combative spirit at home," or "My kids might conclude that they can actually talk with me about what is really happening in their lives.")

_____

_____

_____

_____

Don't expect the impact of your decreased control to be immediate or perfectly satisfying. It takes time for new habits to take root and generate improved reactions. Do expect, though, that your willingness to relinquish the illusion of control will result in less tense and painful anger. The entire family can surely benefit from such an adjustment.

For Family Discussion

1. Begin the discussion by allowing the children to identify moments when they feel their parents are too controlling. You parents can then state the risks you feel are at stake in those circumstances.

2. Have each family member examine his or her own anger. Have each person identify how he or she communicates anger in a controlling fashion.

3. Discuss the role of consequences. Have each person explain why he or she believes it is fair to have positive or negative consequences, depending on the level of responsibility shown.

4. Let each family member take a turn to define freedom. Then discuss what is good about freedom and what is risky about freedom.

5. Have each family member identify how anger communication is improved by choosing not to speak coercively.

6. By allowing greater freedom, you assume that each individual considers personal responsibility more seriously. Have each person describe what he or she believes is a fair expectation when a family member freely chooses to be irresponsible.

For Further Reflection

The story of Adam and Eve's fall into sin is recorded in Genesis 3:1–6. Verse 5 records the temptation that if they ate of the Tree of Knowledge of Good and Evil, they would "be as God." The craving for control began that fateful day and has been ongoing since.

1. How do you seek to "be as God" over your children, to the extent that you attempt to exert too much control? How does this influence the mood of anger in your home?

2. How do your children attempt to control you? What emotional responses does this trigger in you?

3. What types of anger communication would you expect to see in a household that is typified by an ongoing battle for control? Why do the participants continue their efforts to control even when history shows that it does not work?

John 8:31–32 records the words of Jesus: "If you abide in my word then you are truly disciples of mine; and you shall know the truth and the truth shall make you free."

4. Define the freedom that comes from abiding in God's truth. How do unhealthy anger choices leave you feeling entrapped?

5. Healthy anger choices become natural to you only as you allow yourself the freedom to make both good and bad choices. Why is this? What will improve in your own anger management as you allow yourself the full spectrum of choices when you feel angry?

6. Your children possess free will. In the formative years they need guidance to use their freedom wisely. How can you tell when you as a parent are willing to let your children exercise free choice? What seems risky about letting your kids have choices? How will your emotional pitch be different if you speak less controllingly and allow more freedom?

6

THE STRUGGLE FOR SUPERIORITY

STEP 6: Refuse to lord over your child, but speak instead as one who believes in the equal worth of each family member.

There is a good reason angry parents have a hard time letting go of controlling behavior. They mistakenly assume that the best way to be taken seriously is to speak from a position of superiority. If they remind their children who is at the top of the ladder and who is at the bottom, so the reasoning goes, then they win. The communication of anger, then, is not necessarily for the purpose of preserving good values and convictions but to establish the upper hand so there is no question in the underling's mind who is in the more important position.

In the family hierarchy, the parent is indeed in the authority position, while the children are in a more dependent role thanks to their incomplete mental and social development. It would be easy to conclude, then, that the parents are superior and the children are inferior. It is our belief, however, that when parents go into battle to remind the children of their superior position they miss a crucial truth. Having the greater wisdom or being in the decision maker's position does not equate to superiority. The parental role is one of greater responsibility, but this is not to say that parents are superior to their children. They are simply in a different role.

Before God, all persons, young or old, parent or child, are equal. The function of each person within the family system can vary greatly, yet it would be false to assume that one member of the family has greater worth than another. If this truth is forgotten, then communication of anger becomes little more than competition to determine who is more powerful.

In writing the letter of I Corinthians, the apostle Paul was aware that there was great posturing among the church members. Different factions believed they had the proper understanding of life, and therefore the rest should acquiesce and live according to their version of truth. Wanting to put a halt to such thinking, Paul explained that each person brought to the church body differing skills and perspectives. He then made the analogy of a human body. Not all members of the body could be expected to function as a head, nor could all be expected to have the same use as an ear or a hand or an eye. (See I Corinthians 12:4–12.) His point was that it is ill advised for anyone to look down upon those who are in a different position in God's family. We are each unique in function and position, but equal in value before God.

The same insight can be applied to human families. Fathers and mothers and sons and daughters all have different roles within the family unit, and it is best that respect be given to all as they function within their respective roles. At the same time, it is inappropriate to value one member over another to the extent that a false superiority is ascribed to anyone within the system. Paul summarizes this thinking by stating that "there should be no division in the body, but that the members should have the same care for one another" (I Corinthians 12:25).

Sandra was a late-thirties mom with short-cropped blonde hair and a down-to-business way of communicating. After attending one of Dr. Carter's anger workshops at the clinic, she asked if she could speak privately with him about some ongoing problems at home. She had a nine-year-old daughter with ADD, Hannah, and a fourteen-year-old daughter, Bethany. In describing each she explained: "They couldn't be any more different. If no one knew the facts, they would readily assume that they couldn't be sisters. Hannah is dark haired and it looks like she's always going to have a weight problem. She's not interested in socializing and she'd rather stay to herself, or maybe with one other child. Bethany is blonde like me and she's skinny as a rail. She's always been the social organizer since her preschool days, and she's as extroverted as her sister is introverted."

Sandra had anger issues with each of her girls, and by her own description "There is a lot of yelling in our home." She described how Hannah could be quite sullen and moody, and she was terribly disorganized. She could often be described as being "in a fog," and when conflicted she seemed hard to reach. This agitated Sandra greatly; whenever her younger daughter went into her shell, the yelling would begin. "What is *wrong* with you, young lady? How can we ever function like a family if you just withdraw and say nothing? You *cannot* continue being so moody!" Of course, this did nothing to create good feelings between the two.

At the core of Sandra's anger toward Hannah was a reasonable message. She was offended by her daughter's withdrawal tendencies and was indicating that she wanted a more open style of conflict management. Her method of communicating the anger left much to be desired, though. Instead of assertively addressing their problems and maintaining a high regard for her child, in her angry moments Sandra would speak as if Hannah were of lower value. She would become too puffed up, which caused her to speak down to her child.

Has this ever happened to you? In what circumstances have you spoken down to your children? (For instance, "I can become berating when my daughter repeatedly ignores my requests for cooperation," or "I become condescending when I'm talking to my son about our conflicting schedule needs.")

_____

_____

_____

What methods of communication do you most commonly use when you are speaking down to your children? (For instance, "I yell and leave no room for a different perspective," or "I ask questions that are loaded with guilt.")

_____

_____

_____

Indeed, the drive to establish superiority is quite common whenever anger is experienced between parents and their young. Perhaps you have noticed that you are not the only one who uses anger for this purpose. Your children can join in the competition and seem quite determined not to be deemed inferior, as they retort with their own efforts to gain the upper hand.

When Hannah was on the receiving end of Sandra's condescending comments, she often chose to respond to her mother with an "I'll show you" attitude. For instance, Sandra would try to shame her and Hannah might sarcastically reply with, "You don't even know what you're talking about." This was a simple invalidating statement that implied to her mother that she would not succumb to her authority because she knew better. In other words, the daughter was saying, "I'm not going to let you lord over me because my reasoning is actually higher than yours!"

How do your children attempt to show superiority over you? (For instance, "My daughter is a master at pointing out the flaws in my thinking," or "My son can act as if he's too good to have to adhere to my rules; he's aloof.")

_____

_____

_____

Several behaviors are common in people who are making the effort to establish their superiority. Look over this list to determine which behaviors are common in you and in your children. You might place the person's initials next to the applicable statements.

_____ Arguing specifically for the purpose of making the other person's reasoning look foolish.

_____ Speaking forcefully in the hope that your message will silence or shame the other person.

_____ Withdrawing in silence as if to say the other person isn't worth the effort to communicate.

_____ Listening for the purpose of finding fault in the other person's reasoning.

_____ Practicing one-up communication. When the other person says something distasteful, you think of a counterthought that is more distasteful.

_____ Stubbornly refusing to admit wrong, even when it is obvious.

_____ Being so overpowering in communicating convictions that it leaves no room for differing perspectives.

_____ Refusing to accept others' shortcomings, as if you have no shortcomings of your own.

_____ Being stubborn, making no allowance for the idea that other thoughts can be valid.

_____ Being more critical than encouraging.

Attempting to establish superiority can play out in many ways, so this list is not exhaustive. Nonetheless, it can help you begin developing an awareness of this tendency. If you relate to five or more of these traits, it is an indication that you are routinely seeking to be superior. Your anger communications are likely to produce great frustration for all.

A Cover for Inferiority

Why do family members become caught in the trap of managing their anger as an attempt to be superior? Inevitably, the drive for superiority is in direct proportion to a person's deeper conflict with feelings of inferiority. In the effort to appear one-up, the person is in effect saying, "I can't tolerate the thought of being deemed unworthy by my own family member. I must make it very clear that I cannot be treated as a lowly person." Such a thought is often subconscious and influences personal choices in such a lightning-quick way that it may not be exposed. Even so, the fear of being deemed inferior is virtually always behind the drive to be superior.

Think about the things your children do that trigger your anger. What message do you receive? For instance, when Hannah refuses to speak to Sandra, she is insinuating that her mother isn't worth the time or effort. Likewise, when she defiantly challenges Sandra's instructions, it is as if she has concluded that her mother's rationale is so lowly that she will not give her any credence.

Sandra's anger in response to these messages from Hannah was (in part) a way of saying, "I can't let you get away with such lowly opinions toward me. I'm someone to reckon with." Was that anger wrong or misguided? Not really. When children act to insult a parent's worth, it is responsible for the parent to answer with a corrective message. If the parent's anger causes him or her to forget to treat the children with respect, though, it is an indication that the parent is not secure enough to withstand the child's erroneous insults.

How does your anger reflect a deep struggle with feelings of insecurity? (For instance, "I worry that my child thinks so poorly of me that she feels she has the right to insult me," or "All my life I've been frustrated because key family members have rejected me, and when it's my own child who does it as well, it's just more than I can bear.")

_____

_____

_____

_____

Too often, the anger of the parent is a plea wherein the parent is begging the children to have a higher opinion of him or her. For instance, Sandra's anger toward Hannah can be distilled to the questions: "Why is it that you think so poorly of me? What's so awful about my thoughts that causes you to belittle me as you do?" She may not actually say those words, but this is the covert message.

In discussing this matter with Sandra, Dr. Carter wanted her to grapple with the hidden triggers that caused her to be harmful in her angry reaction toward her girls. "Let's agree that there are good reasons for you to feel angry when your own daughters are disrespectful toward you," he began. "It's understandable that you would want to address such an issue. The strength of your anger can be so disproportionate to the circumstance, though, that it makes me wonder what kind of pain is causing such a reaction."

Sandra's face became flushed as the doctor's comments penetrated her mind. "I wish I could tell you that all's well inside me, but it's not," she replied. "My own mother was a difficult person to deal with when I was Hannah and Bethany's age. I never felt like she cared about my opinions. I'm not saying that I had a miserable childhood because lots of good things are part of my past. Yet I never really had the full satisfaction of knowing that I was as highly regarded as I felt I should be."

Then she added, "When I got married I was very optimistic that Jeff and I could have a really special love and that we would be best friends. I'm a very loyal person, and I live with the conviction that if I treat you right surely you will do the same in return. My marriage to Jeff isn't awful, but it's not what I had once dreamed. He has a temper sometimes, and at other times he can go off into his private world and I feel as if I'm nowhere in his thoughts.

"When I became a mom," she continued, "I had this vision that I'd be a confidante to my girls and that we'd enjoy talking and sharing our dreams with each other. But I've learned that they don't necessarily share that same vision. They're getting old enough now that they're exhibiting separate preferences and ideas. Each time one of my girls argues with me, it's like it's a mini-rejection. All my life I've tried so hard to behave appropriately, but I don't seem to have anyone who believes in me the way I try to believe in them. It all makes me wonder if there's something wrong with me."

It is quite common to learn that the anger parents express toward their children is tied to other struggles to feel adequate that originated elsewhere. In Sandra's case, she felt less than appreciated by both her mother and her husband. Both were in the position of helping her to become anchored in security and confidence, yet in Sandra's opinion they had let her down.

What experiences of rejection or disappointment have you had in your past that contribute to your feelings of inadequacy? (For instance, "I've been divorced and I feel labeled by some of my friends as unfit," or "My older brothers constantly put me down, and to this day I still have doubts about the decisions I make.")

_____

_____

_____

How can you know that these unfinished emotions are playing a role in how you manage your anger as a parent? (For instance, "I can see that my child's stubbornness reminds me of the stand-offs I used to have with my own mother," or "I'll yell at my son, but I won't raise my voice with many other people; it seems that I'm unloading my anger onto him because I can get away with it. He's just a convenient target.")

_____

_____

_____

When we talk with parents about managing anger correctly, we remind them that domination does not need to be the ultimate goal. Proving that you are a force to be reckoned with is not necessary. Standing firmly for your needs and convictions is good, although in the process it is wise to uphold the dignity of the person provoking the anger.

A Mind of Equality

To keep your anger exchanges with your kids from resembling a one-up, one-down competition, it is best to remember that in role differences each person has equal value. As the parent you can assume that you have superior logic or wisdom, but you can still communicate with your children with the realization that you do not possess superior worth. If you lord over your children with a superior manner, one of two patterns will emerge. Either the kids learn to think of themselves as truly inferior or they look for ways to counter your communication with an attitude of false superiority.

Jesus once spoke a parable (recorded in Matthew 20:1–16) about workers who were hired by a land owner to work his fields. As the day passed, he would hire new laborers. Even in the last hour of the day, he brought in new workers. When time came to pay the laborers, the land owner gave each person a full day's wage. When those who worked the entire day complained, the owner replied that he had been fair to them, and if he wished to pay the others as one who had worked an equal amount, that was his prerogative. The chief complaint of the day-long workers was: "you have made them equal to us" (verse 12). Jesus' message was clear. Individuals differ in position and function, but God still wants them all to understand that they are equal in his mind.

Sandra was quite somber as she reflected with Dr. Carter about the need to change her communication of anger to indicate an attitude of equality. "I never really considered that I was engaging my girls in a battle for superiority," she admitted. "But once you put my eyes onto it, the pattern is as clear as day. Once I go into a confrontation with either one of them, it's like we are each trying to put the other person's ego down for the purpose of gaining an edge. That's twisted!"

"I'm glad you can see it," the doctor replied, "because that means you can learn to shift gears altogether and communicate with Hannah and Bethany as if they're your equals. They may not have equal wisdom as compared to yours, but they do have an equal need to be treated respectfully."

To communicate anger from a position of equality, there are several adjustments you can make. Let's take a look at some of them.

Realize That Winning Is Not the Goal

How many times have you felt that your conversations with your kids are a debate or a struggle for the higher ground? You can engage in this type of warfare with your kids, and you may even succeed in winning the battle by emphasizing your authority. Yet in the end, what have you really won?

This was the question that prompted Sandra to make some major adjustments when she and her girls felt angry. "Even when I succeed in shutting down Bethany or Hannah," she acknowledged to the doctor, "I can't say that it produces any feeling of satisfaction. Those girls are a part of me, so when they lose, I do too. There's no winning in our angry exchanges."

"Let's spring-board from that thought," replied Dr. Carter, "and determine the better alternative to winning your arguments. First, I suppose you'll have to decide that if winning is not your goal, what is?"

"Well, I guess my goal is to communicate truth, or to express a perspective that they need to incorporate." Sandra was clearly trying to rethink her purpose for expressing anger.

"That sounds good to me," came the reply. "Your challenge is to keep an even tone of voice and refrain from coercion so your goal can be more readily attained."

As an example, Sandra was truly vexed one weekend when she learned that Bethany had lied to her about her whereabouts on a Friday night. She told her mother she would be at a movie with a girlfriend, when in fact she and the friend spent time with two older boys, unchaperoned, at the home of one of the boys. Sandra was emotionally wound tight, but she remembered that winning was not her goal as she spoke with her daughter. Conveying truth was her goal.

Mustering all the self-restraint possible, Sandra spoke with an even tone: "Bethany, I'm assuming you told me the lie because you knew I wouldn't approve of your real plans, and you were right. I'm very disappointed, and I'm going to have to think about the consequences you will need to experience."

"But Mom," came the whiny retort, "we didn't do anything wrong. How can you be so close-minded?"

Sandra chose not to enter the game of one-upmanship at that point, so she stayed on an even keel. "It's plain and simple. If you lie and act contradictory to my plans, there will be consequences. You know that's the way it works."

Again Bethany protested and suggested that her mother was unfair, yet Sandra chose to remain calm but firm. She was beginning to realize that if she went into condescending or shaming mode, she would be entering the battle for superiority. Because Bethany predictably did not want to be in the inferior position, it would lead to the kind of power struggle that always ended badly. Sandra recognized that she could avert that struggle by standing upon her truth without engaging adversarially.

How about you? When might you choose to drop the win-lose style of communication, opting instead for a straightforward approach with your child? (For instance, "If my son tells me I don't know what I'm talking about, I'm not required to explain why my ways are higher than his," or "When my daughter tries to point out the holes in my reasoning, I can stand firmly and I don't have to argue about the errors in her logic.")

_____

_____

_____

_____

How do you suppose this nonadversarial approach will affect your child's response of anger? (For instance, "My son wouldn't like it at first as he realized I won't enter the battle, but he'd probably just fume for a while," or "My daughter is very strong-willed, and she'll keep trying to bait me for an argument.")

_____

_____

_____

_____

As the parent, you are already in the so-called higher position, in the sense that your role carries with it a built-in authority. Each time you engage in a battle to prove that you are indeed above the child, you lose a portion of that natural authority. Stand upon your reasonable ideas, and choose not to turn your disciplining moments into an effort to conquer your child's mind.

Don't Exchange Insult for Insult

With anger existing between you and your children, there is a high probability that they will not yet manage their anger maturely. They are much more likely to use the situation as an opportunity to decipher what is wrong with you, the parent. They may roll their eyes at you or try to point out your illogic or explain that they know a better way to handle the situation. This is caused by their yearning to get out of the underling role and have a greater say in the decisions affecting their lives. They display their immature thinking, however, as they try to get away from the underling role by putting *you* there.

Rather than playing along with the child's illogical tactics, it becomes your task to stay out of the game altogether. By speaking to the child in a reasoned manner with no condescension, you can illustrate what equal-to-equal communication looks like. Be prepared for your children to require much time in learning how to speak with you in an equal fashion. Patience is your valued ally as you choose to be reasonable even when the children are not.

In what circumstances do your children try to bring you down with insults or invalidation? (For instance, "Any time I give my daughter an instruction, she huffs and gripes about how ridiculous my ideas are," or "My son often chooses to do whatever he wants to do, as if my words mean nothing to him.")

_____

_____

_____

Can you see that your children at that moment are trying to elevate themselves by insulting your thoughts? Children make the mistaken assumption that subordination is the same as inferiority. Adults know differently, that subordination is required in any organization as each person in a group is at some time or other required to set aside personal preferences for the good of the group at large. When adults respond to children's efforts to be in the superior portion with force or condescension, they are using the very tactics they want their children not to use.

As your teenagers develop, it is both good and normal for them to want to think separately from you. They are at a stage of life where they are trying to determine who they are and what they believe. This means they will not be shy about questioning your reasoning. Your delicate task is to allow them to have their unique ideas, even as you attempt to maintain an atmosphere of harmony.

Dr. Carter explained to Sandra, "I can fully appreciate how you do not want Hannah or Bethany to communicate toward you as if you were some moron to be disrespected. You don't want them to think it's OK to talk to you as if they hold some superior edge. That's a normal parental desire. As you reprimand them, more than just telling them the better way to act, you have to illustrate what respectfulness looks like. You want them to recognize that talking to someone in a devaluing manner is wrong. Even with differing ideas or desires, they learn that family members can still acknowledge the value of each individual."

What adjustments might you be required to make as you seek not to respond to your child's condescension with more condescension? (For instance, "I'll need to keep a look of respect on my face instead of a look of disdain," or "I can explain consequences to my son without talking to him as if he is a nuisance to me.")

_____

_____

_____

_____

Plan for Equality in Advance

Refraining from insults and speaking with calm firmness requires self-restraint on your part. It means you cannot afford to let your anger be pushed along by quick impulse or pure reflexive response. Your method of addressing frustrations has to be thought out well in advance. To help yourself in this advanced planning, be vigilant regarding the most common scenarios in your home that suck you into the game of one-up, one-down communication.

Proverbs 17:14 states that "the beginning of strife is like releasing water; therefore stop contention before a quarrel starts." Once you open the flood-gates of anger, it is impossible to take back the harm done. The best way to cease the battle for superiority is to not engage in it in the first place.

As an example, Sandra was able to list these circumstances that brought out her vulnerability toward this tendency:

• Hannah would often zone out in front of the TV and ignore her mother's requests. Rather than responding as if she were being insulted, Sandra determined she could turn off the television and make her request with a normal tone of voice.

• It was not uncommon for Hannah to forget to tell her mother about school assignments, meaning there was too much last-minute scrambling to get projects done. Sandra decided that instead of going into the guilt-induction mode, she would carefully go over each of Hannah's school subjects at night and maintain discipline with positive or negative consequences.

• Bethany was prone to complaining about common teenaged issues: what social outings she could attend, movies that would be appropriate, who she should be with, clothing choices. Sandra predetermined that instead of debating Bethany about these items, she would openly discuss the merits of each decision, listening carefully while making no invalidating remarks. She could still set her fourteen-year-old's boundaries, but it would be done without coercion or pleading.

• Whenever Bethany made poor decisions behind her mother's back, Sandra predetermined that she would not reply with shock or scorn. Instead she could say something like: "Looks as if you chose to express your disagreement with me in a hidden fashion. You realize, I suppose, that there will be consequences." In response to the predictable protests, she would not engage in a verbal battle over the correctness of her ideas.

If your family life is like most, your conflicts probably have predictable and repetitive themes. What circumstances are most likely to invite the one-up, one-down form of communication? (For instance, "Our disagreements about my son's choice of friends," or "Discussions about my teenager's more permissive social preferences.")

_____

_____

_____

Decide in advance how you would like to handle the frustrations in those circumstances, particularly when your children try to hold their reasoning higher than yours. What adjustments can you make to show your belief in your child's equal worth, even as you address the problem openly? (For instance, "When my son tells me that I don't trust him and that I live in the Dark Ages, I can choose not to debate at that moment," or "I can remember what it felt like to be corrected when I was the same age as my daughter, and I can speak with the same respectfulness I would have liked.")

_____

_____

_____

We are suggesting that it is risky to let your conflict management style hinge on angry words spoken impulsively. Great forethought is required in keeping your expressions from being harmful, but the results can prove to be quite rewarding.

Find What Is Right in Your Child's Perspective

When your child is angry with you, even if that anger becomes part of an attempt to appear superior, there may be a valid notion in your child's mind. Even if you can find little that seems valid, remember that the child still thinks he or she has a reasonable perspective. One of the goals of equal-to-equal communication is establishment of respect. Since children are likely to model their behavior on their observation of you, it is good for you to show what it is like to be attentive.

For instance, when Bethany lied to Sandra about the evening she spent time with the older boys, Sandra was rightly concerned that her daughter could be exposed to temptations she was not prepared to handle. As the mother, she could become so focused on getting her message out to her daughter that she would easily overlook her daughter's perspective. Instead of going into a scolding form of communication, which would be received by Bethany as a putdown (placing her in the inferior position), Sandra could speak as one equal to another by showing her daughter that she comprehended the girl's perspective.

An equal form of communication might have gone like this: "Bethany, I know what it's like to want the approval of guys, particularly when you see a lot in them that looks attractive. Let's talk about what drew you in toward them." She could continue with further comments: "I'm sure it makes you feel childish when you have to expose that you've got restrictions on you that your peers may not have. I'm willing to talk about that with you and I hope you'll be willing to hear my concerns about unchaperoned time with older guys."

Sandra could still hold to her principles, and she could still apply consequences if needed, but it would not have to be accompanied by an "I'll show you who's boss" attitude.

What is it that your children seem to want you to understand most about them? (For instance, "My daughter wants me to know how important peer acceptance is," or "My son is genuinely turned off by subjects at school that seem irrelevant to him.")

What is it that you want most for your children to understand about you? (For instance, "I want my son to realize that when I insist on developing good habits, I'm looking out for his best interests," or "I want my daughter to realize that I know what I'm talking about when I put restrictions on her weekend activities.")

How might your willingness to accept your child's perspective (even if it seems clearly wrong) lead to a more productive exchange when tension might easily be high? (For instance, "By my open-mindedness I can set the example worth being followed," or "When I'm even-handed it tends not to create a war of words.")

_____

_____

_____

_____

When you refrain from the temptation to elevate yourself by putting your child down, you will never be required to let go of your good convictions or cease from being a disciplinarian. Rather, you illustrate that angry feelings can be openly processed while also maintaining a high regard for the other person. Your children may be slow, sometimes painfully slow, in joining you with this style of thought, but even if it takes years for them to join you in communicating as one equal to another you still gain. Your anger will be tempered and your reputation inside the home will be fair.

As you succeed in communicating from a position of equality, you have the credibility to teach them about the love of God that transcends rank or achievement.

For Family Discussion

1. Have each family member identify how the other family members attempt to be superior in their reasoning. Then have each person admit how they make counterattempts to establish superiority.

2. With each family member participating, discuss this question: "How does the attitude of superiority affect the level of anger in each of us?"

3. Have each person answer the question: "In what circumstances do you find yourself struggling with feelings of inferiority or insecurity?" Then have each person discuss how such feelings might increase the tendency to feel angry.

4. Though family roles differ, each individual is of equal value. Let each family member express to each of the other individuals how he or she would feel if consistently treated with equal value.

5. Have each individual speculate how conflict would be handled more appropriately if he or she chose not to win or conquer.

6. Have each person respond to this question: "How is your anger affected when the other person clearly attempts to show understanding for your perspective?"

For Further Reflection

Proverbs 30:32 gives interesting guidance: "If you have been foolish in exalting yourself or if you have plotted evil, put your hand on your mouth."

1. How might parents foolishly exalt themselves above their children? Why do we parents attempt to show our superiority?

2. If your children sense that you are holding yourself in a superior manner, it can send the message that you see them as inferior. How might a child respond to such a message? How might a child attempt to establish a position of superiority?

Proverbs 30:33 continues with an analogy: "For the churning of milk produces butter and the pressing of the nose brings forth blood; so the churning of anger produces strife."

3. It is certain that the battle for supremacy perpetuates strife. Why do many parents continue to strive for dominance even though disastrous results are so predictable?

I Peter 3:8 says: "Let all be harmonious, sympathetic, brotherly, kind-hearted, and humble in spirit."

4. Winning is not the goal when you confront your children; harmony is a better aim. How does the tone of your anger change for the better if you keep the goal of harmony in mind? In what way can you address anger-provoking circumstances even as you maintain a spirit of kind-heartedness?

I Peter 3:9 instructs that we not return evil for evil or insult for insult.

5. How do your conflicts at home resemble a struggle to be one-up? When your children seemingly want to engage you in a battle for the upper hand, how can you bring sanity to the situation by refraining from the temptation to respond to insult with insult?

6. What does it mean when we say that family members are different in roles yet equal in value? How is your communication of anger affected if you consider your children to have equal value?

7

ANGER AS AN EGO TRIP

STEP 7: Let humility be your guide as you demonstrate
to your children that selfishness has no place
in successful anger management.

At the core of every personality is the characteristic of self-absorption. This is not a flattering statement, but, observing people will reveal this trait.

Each person contends inwardly with the sin nature, and it is this struggle that produces the trait of self-absorption. We are each driven toward unhealthy behavior because our sinfulness compels us to ignore what we know to be wise and godly, as we opt instead to follow the paths of self-centeredness. In any episode of family conflict, each participant struggles mightily to push the self's agenda, ignoring altogether the needs and feelings of others. So consumed are we by egocentric thoughts that we quickly discard any awareness of the need for fair play or harmonizing. Can you relate?

Let's go back and revisit Sandra, introduced in the preceding chapter. Her nine-year-old daughter, Hannah, was quiet, stubborn, and disorganized, while fourteen-year-old Bethany was much more expressive and extroverted. Sandra tried hard to be a calming influence when they quarreled or when they struggled with the typical problems associated with their ages, yet she would sometimes forget the coaching she had received in counseling and she would use anger nonproductively. Predictably, she began expressing great frustration with herself.

She told Dr. Carter: "I really feel motivated when I leave your office and go back home to face my girls. I actually try to anticipate what might cause me to become angry, and I will even rehearse mentally how I could respond. But when those two start with their sarcasm or defiance, I throw all my good intentions right out the window! I don't know what gets into me in those moments, but in spite of my good intentions, I lose it."

"Let's take a hard look at one of the least pleasant ingredients in human personality," Dr. Carter replied. "Would you be willing to admit that each time you express your anger wrongly, there is a degree of selfishness at work?"

"A degree? I think there's a lot more than just a degree of selfishness," she answered. "Sometimes I feel like I'm so full of my right ideas that I'm incapable of seeing anything else. So yes, I think this is something that's definitely in play."

Think about some of your recent incidents of anger with your children. Perhaps your son defied your ground rules regarding curfew, or maybe you learned that your daughter made poor grades because she was not preparing for her classes despite her assurances that she was on top of things. Try to recall the thoughts you nursed in your mind as your anger built. Perhaps you can recognize key sentiments:

"Why do I have to put up with this ongoing irresponsibility?"
"This child is giving me fits."
"No matter how clearly I communicate, this kid won't listen to me."
"I'm tired of all the hassles."
"I can't stand it when I'm not taken seriously."
"What do I have to say or do to get through to this child?"

You may notice that it is easy to put the focus back onto yourself, fretting about the inconvenience or annoyance that has been stimulated in you. How might your anger be fueled by thoughts that focus on the inconvenience your child creates for yourself? (For instance, "In the mornings before school, I get easily annoyed with my daughter because she won't listen to me as I prod her to get ready," or "I can dwell on the hurt of knowing that my son rarely takes me seriously when I try to teach him about discipline.")

_____

_____

_____

Shift gears now, and focus on the anger being experienced by your child. How does he or she focus so heavily on personal preferences that your thoughts are ignored? (For instance, "My daughter can be so focused on her social needs that she rarely factors in the needs of the family," or "My son cares about no one's opinion other than his own.")

_____

_____

_____

Defining Pride

Whenever anger is mismanaged, you do not have to look far to find that prideful emotions are strongly influencing how the anger is managed. Pride can be defined as a preoccupation with one's preferences, cravings, or desires. It prompts individuals to be much more focused on personal needs than on the needs of others. In fact, when pridefulness is engaged, there is little inclination to consider the perspectives of others. Self is on center stage.

Self-centeredness has qualities that are acquired through experience, but it is a trait so indigenous to human nature that it dwells in each individual from the earliest moments of life. It is not a learned trait; it is inborn. Recall when your children were mere toddlers. Did you ever witness them acting in self-centered ways? Did they ever display anger because they did not receive what they wanted? With no training at all, children naturally observe the world with a mind-set that is focused on self. "What have you done for me lately?" "How can I get you to do what I want?" "I insist that things should go my way." These are the sentiments that are at the base of a young child's reasoning. It would be nice for little children to be more inclined to consider the feelings and needs of others, and occasionally they are. The sin nature has such a grip on each person, though, that it is far more likely a little children is consumed less with others than with self.

As the years progress, children learn to factor in the needs of others. When this happens, we say that the child is maturing. Yet even as the maturation process unfolds, it continues to be natural to fall back into the self-oriented way of responding. By the time children reach the adult years, we hope that self-absorption will disappear. Nonetheless, it never happens, meaning that adults (who eventually take on the parental roles) continue to have self-absorbed thoughts. That tendency, then, is in play whenever they address their children, who are naturally self-absorbed, and the cycle goes on, generation after generation.

Do you recall the first time your children handled anger with pridefulness leading the way? (For instance, "My son was the most stubborn toddler you ever saw, and it was a battle to get him to obey," or "From the earliest years, my daughter would tune me out as if I did not even exist.")

_____

_____

_____

In those early years as a parent, how would your pridefulness take over your management of anger? (For instance, "I really struggled with impatience because my son was so easily agitated," or "I would become very insistent, to the extent that I might hurt my child's feelings.")

_____

_____

_____

To minimize the effect of pridefulness on your style of handling anger, it is helpful to develop a broad awareness of its influence. Our experience tells us pride is at the base of every negative trait in the human personality—it is that pervasive. It is easy, for instance, to identify how pride is at the center of many openly annoying qualities. You can spot it in traits such as criticism, impatience, harsh communication, blaming, lying, speaking insults, fretting, making demands, and interrupting. If you break down each of these traits, you discover at the base that the person is thinking something along the lines of "I cannot rest until I get what I want."

How is your pride displayed in this openly agitating behavior? (For instance, "When I'm not taken seriously I shout and intimidate," or "Once it's clear that my kids won't be cooperative, I act impatiently.")

_____

_____

_____

How about your children? How do they display pridefulness through open behavior of this sort? (For instance, "My daughter becomes openly sassy when I don't give her what she wants," or "My son gripes about never being able to do what he wants.")

_____

_____

_____

Not only is pridefulness at the base of loud or openly agitated behavior, it appears during more passive forms of protest as well. See if you can spot its presence in these traits: stubbornness, withdrawal, evasiveness, chronic forgetfulness, tuning out, ignoring, making promises but with no follow-up, quitting, being painfully slow, and refusing to think on a deep level. In each of these behaviors, the choice is made to allow the self's needs to supersede those of anyone else. Harmony is lost since there is little or no teamwork being considered.

Do you ever find yourself so self-preoccupied that you display pride in one or more of these passive behaviors? Which ones are common in you? (For instance, "When I am fed up with the kids, I may withdraw for long stretches of time," or "I have become so angry at my son that I will refuse to help him on any tasks he wants done.")

_____

_____

_____

What about your children? How do they exhibit self-absorption in a passive or subtle way? (For instance, "My daughter sometimes acts like a zombie, and she can be oblivious that others are even in her presence," or "My son is sneaky, to the extent that there are times when I can hardly tell if he is being truthful or not.")

_____

_____

_____

When pridefulness attaches to anger, there may be a reasonable message that needs to be expressed, but because it has such an egocentric slant it is likely to be lost. What is it about your ego-driven anger that does not get through to your kids? (For instance, "It's right that I want cooperation, but my method of communication can be so haughty that my children feel rejected," or "My pridefulness keeps me from hearing my daughter when we're at odds with each other.")

_____

_____

_____

_____

Sandra spoke with Dr. Carter about this new awareness. "I've always been able to admit that I could be selfish at times, but I guess I've never really slowed down long enough to recognize how it plays such a powerful role in my anger. Just this week I was angry at Bethany because she is so uncooperative when I monitor her school projects. I could easily point out to her how she has a snooty approach toward me, but right when I was in the middle of fussing at her, it dawned on me that I was displaying the very self-centered style of communication that I dislike in her. I was acting impatiently and was hyperfocused on what I wanted her to do for me."

"Each time you and your girls have a conflict," said Dr. Carter, "they are taking mental notes regarding how you handle your own emotions. I'm sure you are painfully aware of how selfish they can be as they talk with you. I know it can be pressure for you, but your task is to show them what unselfish anger looks like. You have good ideas to offer them, so if you match your good message with a self-restrained spirit, you may make some headway."

Sandra smiled sheepishly as she said, "I guess no one said counseling would be easy."

Humility and Anger

The issue of pridefulness is put into perspective in I Peter 5:5: "God is opposed to the proud, but gives grace to the humble." The opposite of pride is humility. In his years of ministry with Jesus, Peter surely noticed that Jesus did nothing from an egotistical motive. His consistent focus was to live in a manner that reflected God's goodness, and he understood that godliness meant he would have to set his own cravings aside long enough to factor in the needs and feelings of others. This was something that Jesus did with no begrudging or obligation.

If pridefulness is identifiable by its self-absorption, humility is typified by a lack of self-absorption. In humility, you still have a need to openly address anger-provoking circumstances, but you do so with a servant's heart. You can begin with the realization that your children will not necessarily give you full credibility, yet that reality does not have to prompt you to thump your chest or demand your rights. You could recognize instead that parenting requires a large dose of self-restraint, applied for years. Even as you want to guide your children toward your values, it is not done with a you-owe-it-to-me mentality. Instead, your primary thought might be something like "I care enough about you to show you the way to good habits."

To get an idea of how humility is displayed, look over this list of traits for this quality:

- The ability to slow down long enough to consider the other person's perspective
- Being respectful even as you maintain firmness
- Recognition that your needs are not always the most pressing matter
- Setting aside selfishness long enough to display a team spirit

- Maintaining patience when the young person does not agree with your perspective
- Listening having priority over telling
- Servitude as a highly prized trait
- Confronting with a spirit of love, not spitefulness
- The willingness to understand another person's feelings, no matter how odd they may seem
- Letting go of the need to always be right

As you consider the quality of humility, what is it about this trait that could be most beneficial to you? (For instance, "I could be less self-absorbed when responding to my kids' needs," or "I can establish leadership by my acts of service and fair-mindedness.")

_____

_____

_____

Dr. Carter challenged Sandra to embrace humility as she responded to Bethany and Hannah's moods. "Go ahead and assume," he said, "that for the next several years they will still be inclined to speak in self-absorbed ways. It's not a cheery thought, but that's a very common characteristic among growing kids. When you make room for their less-than-ideal responses, you are prepared to illustrate the better alternative: humility. As a humble parent, you won't insist on perfect responses from them. Instead you can determine to communicate your good perspectives calmly and firmly, with a realization that they may disagree. You may need to explain consequences, yet even then you can do so for their edification, not just for the purpose of getting your way."

"Now you're really asking me to be honest with myself, aren't you?" came her reply. "I guess I'll have to double-check my motives to see if I'm asking for conformity just so my ego will be satisfied, or because my love compels me to be firm." Sandra was right on target!

Think very carefully about the times you've felt frustrated with your children. How can you tell if your admonishment is propelled by a spirit of humility instead of pridefulness? (For instance, "In an attitude of

humility, I'm less degrading," or "If I'm being humble, I'm more inclined to hear my son's perspective even if I feel he is wrong.")

_____

_____

_____

If pridefulness is the beginning of all negative characteristics, it stands
to reason that pride's opposite is the beginning of each positive trait.
Think about many of the healing, godly traits you could apply to conflict, to determine how they are a reflection of humility: patience, kindness, listening, calm, showing respect, forgiving, being constructively
assertive, fair-mindedness, self-restraint, empathy, objectivity. With each
of these traits there is a willingness to set aside the self's preoccupation long enough to consider the other's perspective. To be humble, you
need not give up firmness or discipline. Rather, firmness is accompanied by an attitude of servitude.

Which displays of humility are most helpful when you are in conflict
with your kids? (For instance, "I need to commit to a greater sense of patience," or "I need to recognize that my son's anger reflects a deeper need
for acceptance.")

_____

_____

_____

To exchange pridefulness for humility is no easy task. In fact, if we attempt to act humbly in our own strength, we will surely falter. Recognizing this, the apostle Paul determined that he needed to do nothing
less than consider himself dead. In one of the pivotal verses in the New
Testament, he wrote: "I have been crucified with Christ; it is no longer I
who live, but Christ who lives in me" (Galatians 2:20). So wary was he of
his own capability to be ego-driven, he determined that each day he had
to make a conscious decision to set self's agenda aside in order to yield to
the leading of the Holy Spirit. This meant he would need to studiously discern God's will as it related to each event he encountered.

Parents can find confidence as they regularly take time out to study and know God's will, not just as an intellectual exercise but as it relates to everyday circumstances. This may not always feel easy or natural, but as Sandra learned it can be done. With a determination to yield your priorities to the Holy Spirit and to give highest priority to humility, certain adjustments can be made so your anger is more productive. Let's examine a few.

Determine If Your Expressions Are Good for Both You and Your Child

Being correct can be a dangerous thing. At first glance it may seem like a strange thought, but you should recognize that many episodes of anger gone awry begin with strong sentiments of correctness. Sandra, for example, was correct when she told Bethany not to lie. Yet her correctness "permitted" her to speak so overwhelmingly that the emotions would spiral out of control.

Before addressing problems with your children, be willing to determine if it is truly necessary to confront. You will certainly conclude that there are times when it is good to speak about matters of conflict, but you may also determine that pushing your point is a detriment. Sometimes your confrontations fit the category of finicky preferences, meaning they really do not need to be spoken at all. Other times, you have valid issues to address, but you need to pick and choose your times to confront judiciously. At other times, though, you discern that confronting a problem is the loving thing to do, meaning you decide to put your thoughts on open display.

Sandra really became peeved when she knew Bethany was hedging on the truth. As a teen, Bethany wanted increasing freedom, and that was understandable. As the parent, Sandra wanted reasonable accountability, and that too was valid. In teaching her daughter to be honest about her activities, Sandra was recognizing that she needed to determine when to push her correctness and when not to push. She rightly reasoned that a mind of humility would prompt her to be considerate of her daughter's readiness to receive input.

Bethany asked her mother for some money as she was leaving to meet friends. When Sandra reminded her that she had given her twenty dollars the previous day, Bethany retorted, "You did not." Sandra had no doubt that the exchange occurred, and she knew that her daughter was trying to con her for more money. In the past, Sandra would have tried forcing Bethany to admit she was not being honest, and predictably a loud argument would have ensued. This time, she merely stated, "I have no more money to give you. It looks like you'll need to budget your money better in the future." Bethany was clearly annoyed, yet Sandra wisely realized that she would hold her ground without getting drawn into a heated debate.

Because of your love as a parent, it is good to speak about developing good virtues. Yet your attitude of humility causes you to remember that you are limited in your ability to make your child think like you, that you may not always succeed in bringing your children around to your way of reasoning. If that happens, pridefulness might provoke you to become insistent, not resting until your correctness is acknowledged. Humility, however, prompts you to be patient, knowing that your son or daughter is not on the same level of maturity as you. You remember that parenting is a long-term project and your truths may not be absorbed as quickly as you would like.

When do you have difficulty discerning if your confrontations are right for the moment? (For instance, "When I talk to my daughter about her poor follow-through on tasks, she predictably argues. Often we go round and round about her argumentative demeanor," or "I can't stand it when my son emotionally brushes me off, and I want to make an issue of it every time he does so.")

_____

_____

_____

How would your management of anger differ if you were more judicious in choosing the best time to confront? (For instance, "I wouldn't have to repeatedly try to convince my daughter that her argumentativeness is so annoying," or "When my son brushes me off, it's not necessary to give him a lecture each time about the inappropriateness of his behavior.")

_____

_____

_____

The anger you wish to communicate may not be wrong, but with humility leading the way you can learn not to be so absorbed with your own correctness that you lose the ability to speak with constructive timing.

Make Room for the Child's Poor Reaction

In a perfect world, when you discuss your preferences with your children your words are well received and full harmony is immediately forthcoming. But this is not a perfect world. Because children can be pridefully absorbed in their own desires, it is highly predictable that your ideas will be met with disdain or disagreement. If your pride leads the way in your response to their disagreement, it can prompt you to react something like this: "Who do you think you are to disagree with me?" The thought may be lightning-quick; it causes you to use harsh or nonproductive anger.

How might your anger represent a sense of shock or dismay that your child would dare to disagree with you? (For instance, "Sometimes I explode because I can't believe my son would choose to be as disrespectful as he is," or "It blows my mind each time my daughter tells me she'll do one thing, and then she does the exact opposite.")

_____

_____

_____

When you embrace humility, you make room for the reality that your children can and will disappoint. You are not required to like this reality; however, you can admit that it happens. Appealing to common sense, you might ask yourself how successful your angry exchanges are when you pridefully insist that your children must always respond well to your directions. Of course, you would admit that such an approach not only does not work but is destined to fail miserably.

It would be highly unusual for your children to respond to your wishes each time with a delighted response. So don't delude yourself with the notion that it's supposed to be that way. For instance, children can and will gripe when you tell them no, or when you won't allow their preferred activity every time, or when you direct them to a responsibility that may feel inconvenient to them. It is actually arrogant for parents to assume that their children should think well of every idea spoken to them.

Sandra chuckled in mock amusement as she said to the doctor, "I never really thought I was arrogant if I'd get mad at my girls when they disagreed or talked back. But now that you've pointed it out, it does seem rather absurd to think that my children would always respond to my corrections with a smile." Pausing, she admitted, "I know I didn't always agree with my parents when I was their age."

"Parents can feel as if they're actually condoning their children's disrespect when they don't immediately draw attention to it," said the doctor. "My goal in suggesting that you make room for disagreement, though, is not intended to send them the message that it's OK to be rude or disruptive. Rather, I'm hoping you can stay on track with an accepting demeanor, as opposed to being pulled into a nonproductive argument about your girls' responses."

Hannah was complaining one evening because she wanted to have a guest at their home, but her mother had told her it would not be possible. As Hannah continued griping, Sandra wanted to launch into a lecture about the need for cooperation and her daughter's need to stop complaining every time she did not get her way. Thinking in terms of humility, Sandra reminded herself that in the past lectures only made matters worse. This would be one of those moments to make room for her daughter's bad mood. Calmly, she told Hannah, "I know you're disappointed, but my decision still stands." When Hannah again complained, Sandra spoke in the same tone of voice, "It's not what you want, but that's the decision I've made."

As you display restraint in your convictions, you model to your children how to handle anger in a clean fashion; that is a far more powerful teaching method than a scolding lecture. Sandra did not retreat from her firmness, yet because she did not insist that her daughter must feel wonderful about the decision she was not drawn into a battle sure to produce futility.

In what circumstances do you need to put restraints on your anger as you make room for your children disliking your choices? (For instance, "When my son accuses me of being narrow-minded because of my decision to keep him from a keg party, I can hold my ground without pleading with him to agree with me," or "When my daughter shows displeasure for having to do her homework, I need not draw attention to her moodiness.")

_____

_____

_____

_____

When Pressed into Applying Consequences, Don't Argue

Because you love your children, there may be circumstances that require the application of consequences for their poor choices. Applying discipline can be an act of humility if it means you are willing to uphold loving standards even though they may not be popular at the moment. The decision to discipline often prompts you to set your own need for comfort aside in order to do what is wisest for your child. Your child may not like your choices, but you can find solace in knowing that your choices result in good.

In applying consequences, it is best to do so with your pride in check. When your words become too insistent or when you debate the merits of your opinions, notice what you are indicating. Your argumentativeness says: "I have to be the ultimate around here. I cannot live with the thought that you may assume your opinions are better than mine." You may not say those very words, but this is what your pushy argument may imply.

By applying consequences, one lesson you want your children to learn is that the world does not revolve around them. They cannot expect to make decisions on the assumption that others should just cater to them. This message can be lost, however, if you imply that the world is supposed to revolve around *you*. The more overbearing you are when disciplining, the more competitive the atmosphere becomes. The good message behind the discipline can be overshadowed by ego, which can prompt the child to think, *Maybe you're going to win this round, but I'm determined not to bow to your authority forever.*

Sandra realized how necessary it was to keep pridefulness out of the discipline process with her girls, but she needed help to determine how humility would be displayed as her daughters tried to draw her into the battle. Dr. Carter explained, "Once you've decided upon a consequence, it's predictable that your girls will want to challenge you regarding the validity of your decision. In other words, your ego will be attacked. If you hold firmly to a mind-set of humility, you can remind yourself that your ego is not really of primary concern at the moment. The girls feel hurt or embarrassed, which is why they want to attack you."

"So I'm just supposed to let them get away with insulting or sarcastic words?"

"No, that's why you would be willing to apply consequences," Dr. Carter responded. "That's your way of letting them know that you won't let their egos go unchecked. But even as you hold firm, it's not necessary to get drawn into any debate. Simply let them know that the decision is made and you plan to stick to it."

When do your children try to draw you into a debate over discipline practices? (For instance, "My daughter accuses me of being unfair when I put her on restriction," or "My son is very stubborn, and I constantly feel like he stands in judgment over me.")

_____

_____

_____

_____

What prideful thoughts do you battle with inwardly when your kids try to argue with you? (For instance, "How dare you question my motives?" or "Why is it that I have to put up with this kind of attitude from a child?")

_____

_____

_____

What would be the humble alternative as you respond to your child's brashness? (For instance, "I don't need to convince my son that I'm a force to be reckoned with; he can figure that out on his own," or "I can remind myself that I too had confusion when I tried to come to terms with my own parents.")

_____

_____

_____

Remain Calm Even as the Child Is Not

The net result of a mind-set of humility is that you put your own self-absorption aside long enough to remember that discipline with your children is not an exercise to make you feel important. Discipline is administered because love compels it. In love, you can choose patience, kindness, and a noninsistent spirit. Although these traits may be counter to what you feel at the moment, you can give priority to them despite your momentary mood.

Sandra realized that successful anger management required a great amount of soul searching: "I guess I've been so busy being a reactor when my girls argue with me that I lost my sense of initiative. I don't want my anger to be ego-driven, but that's exactly what happens when I lose my perspective."

Parents can quietly cling to the fantasy that their children will hold them in high regard, and that they will appreciate the thoughts that accompany the parent's decisions. When the parents express anger, it is evidence that the fantasy is prohibiting them from accepting the reality that children can and will be selfish, not appreciative. Calmness comes when parents drop the fantasy and accept the reality that their decisions are not always popular or well received.

When do you find calmness most elusive as you interact with your children? (For instance, "They drive me crazy when they bicker on and on with each other," or "I hate it when my son acts as if he knows better than me.")

_____

_____

_____

What would be the advantage of choosing to keep your calm even as you respond to those circumstances? (For instance, "I would not add to the anger that already exists," or "My confidence would not become an issue when my son becomes angry with me.")

_____

_____

_____

As you make an effort to exchange pridefulness for humility, recognize that it involves a threefold process:

1. Developing an acute awareness of the many ways your pride can goad your anger

2. Being specific as you identify how humility is displayed even as you continue to be firm

3. Letting your behavior become an open reflection of your humble thoughts

Sandra summarized the difficulty of this effort when she told the doctor: "It's easy to theorize about the merits of humility. All my adult life, I've heard about the need to keep my pride in check, and that's something I readily agree with. I guess I never really took the time to scrutinize my anger for the purpose of seeing the pride that keeps it alive. Humility is easy when others join you in the effort. My job now is to choose humility even if my children show no willingness to join in the effort."

When angry moments arise with your children, be aware that they immediately go into the learning mode. Because you want them to learn to manage their anger correctly, you can show them what clean anger looks like. What a humble thought it is to recognize that you are a professor when anger is present!

To succeed in maintaining a humble spirit, it is helpful to learn to be the least defensive. This topic is explored in the next chapter.

For Family Discussion

1. Pride can be both a positive quality and a negative quality. Have each person describe what makes him or her feel proud (in the positive sense). Then have each person describe what the negative form of pride can do.

2. Go around the room and have each person answer these questions: "When are you most likely to think in a self-centered manner? How is your selfishness displayed?"

3. When you think of a humble person, what comes to mind? What are some of the key traits that you would expect to find in a humble person?

4. Have each person identify what he or she would have to give up or change in order to be more committed to the trait of humility.

5. It is difficult to be humble once you begin feeling angry. How can you communicate anger in a humble manner?

6. A humble person can accept another's flaws. In what situations are you most willing to show an accepting spirit toward your family members?

For Further Reflection

James 4:6 reminds us that "God is opposed to the proud but gives grace to the humble."

1. Pride can be demonstrated with a haughty spirit, but it is much broader than that. How might you display a prideful spirit toward your children? How do your children display pridefulness toward you?

2. When you are influenced by your own pridefulness, how does this create an inappropriate response of anger? How do your children respond when it is clear that your self-absorption is on display?

Philippians 2:3 instructs: "Do nothing from selfishness or empty conceit, but with humility of mind let each of you regard one another as more important than himself."

3. What does humility mean to you? How would an attitude of humility guide you when your feelings of anger toward your children are aroused?

4. When handled correctly, assertiveness can be an extension of a mind of humility. How can this be? In what ways are you serving your children when you practice assertiveness?

5. Suppose your children have little or no appreciation for your efforts to be assertive. How does this affect your anger? How can you maintain your resolve to have a mind of humility even while it is scorned or rebuffed?

Proverbs 15:1 tells us, "A gentle answer turns away wrath, but a harsh word stirs up anger."

6. In what circumstances do you need to practice gentleness even as you are faced with your child's wrath? What is the best way to combine gentleness with firmness?

8

DROPPING DEFENSES

STEP 8: Don't be threatened by an adversarial response, but be confident in your own response.

Alan, a man in his mid-forties, sat in Dr. Minirth's office with his sixteen-year-old son, Jeron. Alan had struggled for years with major mood swings and anger outbursts, and with Dr. Minirth's help it was determined that he had bipolar disorder. The doctor explained that without the proper balance of chemistry in the brain, his difficulties with anger would continue. Once the proper medicine was prescribed, Alan's outbursts became less severe and less frequent. Alan brought Jeron in for an evaluation because he too had a tendency toward mood swings.

After interviewing both father and son, and after examining blood lab reports, Dr. Minirth determined that it would be premature to assume that Jeron could also be diagnosed as bipolar. Yes, he could be moody and his anger could have an edge of bitterness, but the doctor had a distinct sense that Jeron's anger patterns were less physiological in origin and more of a reaction to ongoing matters within the home that were unresolved.

As Dr. Minirth came to know Alan and his son, he heard numerous stories involving conflict that created painful emotions. Jeron, for instance, had taken an interest in hard rock groups that spewed anger in their music. Alan would often argue strongly with his son about bringing evil elements into their home, and on several occasions the exchanges became ugly.

Over time, Dr. Minirth noticed a consistent pattern between father and son. Alan, who described himself as a "cut and dried communicator," frequently would shout and curse at his son for making poor choices. Jeron was not as fiery as his dad, but he grew emboldened as he aged, and at this point in their relationship he would often respond to his father's outbursts with his own powerful displays.

Stop and think for a moment about the ease with which family conflict can deteriorate into nonproductive exchanges. When parents and children enter a war of wills, it is common to observe strong defensiveness on both sides. One person speaks accusingly toward the other. The sentiment is not well received, and it elicits a defensive reaction. This response is perceived as an affront, so more forcefulness is forthcoming, and the exchange falls apart rapidly.

Has this ever happened in your communication with your children? When do you find your interaction resembling an offensive-defensive battle? (For instance, "When I correct my son, he invariably has an argumentative response, which causes me to respond argumentatively," or "When I try to talk with my daughter about something that needs to be done, she acts huffy and I make it my business to try to get her to respond correctly; the result is pure tension.")

Anger and conflict are not pleasant occurrences in any family, and this is something few people anticipate with glee. When parents and children experience conflict, they think, "Oh no, here we go again." Immediately, defensiveness becomes a major feature in their exchanges, meaning the anger is probably adversely affected. But it does not have to be this way.

When you and your children respond to each other with defensiveness, it indicates fear. Upon receiving a parent's confrontation, children may fear being rejected or controlled or misunderstood. If they respond poorly, the parent may fear being disrespected, insulted, or ignored. You can detect the presence of fear by recognizing the defensiveness that accompanies it.

Those who are focused on letting the Holy Spirit guide their parenting do not succumb habitually to fearful responses. The psalmist learned the art of appealing to the calming hand of God when faced with adversarial circumstances. "When I am afraid," he recorded in the fifty-sixth psalm, "I will trust in you . . . what can mere man do to me?" (verses 3–4). Rather than immediately flinching with tension in the midst of strain, he would slow himself to consider God's presence and immediate guidance.

Likewise, if parents are faced with an adversarial response from their own family members, they might ask, "What can this person do to me if I am grounded in a reasonable manner of life?" Defensiveness is out, as objectivity is in. Before this shift can be made, however, one must be honest with oneself about the very presence of fear.

Dr. Minirth pointed out to Alan that he and Jeron seemed to let fear gain a foothold whenever they tried to respond to differences. The patient's response was sharp and disagreeable: "Fear! You're suggesting that I'm afraid of my own son? I don't think so!"

"I've noticed that you tend to respond defensively virtually every time your son disagrees. I'm not suggesting that your son is correct to challenge you, but I am suggesting that you seem readily threatened by his challenges. Your anger is an indication that you have major doubts about your son's sentiments, and major doubts about your own ability to handle him with reason."

Alan did not answer out loud, but his defensive reaction revealed an underlying thought along these lines: "Oh no! My son doesn't respect me! This is terrible! What will I do?" His outer words were actually rude or forceful, but his inner spirit was anything but trusting or God-focused.

When people feel fear, it is not always accompanied by cowering behavior or physical retreat. Fear cannot be so easily stereotyped. In fear, anger is often displayed and can seem so prominent that it is easy to overlook the fear dimension. In Chapter Two, we explored the three general ways anger can be mismanaged. Notice how fear can play a role in each one:

- *Suppressed anger.* The person thinks, "If I let my real frustrations become known, it may create more problems than it's worth, and that might be too much for me to handle."
- *Openly aggressive anger.* When being forceful or abrasive in anger, the defensive response could be motivated by a thought such as "I can't let others harbor ideas or perceptions counter to mine. That's too unsettling. I've got to squash differentness before it creates problems that I'm not capable of managing."
- *Passive-aggressive anger.* The subversively angry person may think, "I want to register how displeased I feel, but if I'm too open it might create real difficulties for me. I'd better disguise my anger so it won't put me in a vulnerable position."

When you handle anger in a less-than-desirable way, what fear is in play? (For instance, "When my daughter acts defiantly, I raise my voice and become forceful because I fear that she won't take me seriously if I use a regular tone of voice," or "When I'm arguing with my son it's because I fear that he'll exercise poor judgment, so I have to be extra firm.")

_____

_____

_____

As your children mismanage anger, what fear do you suppose is pushing the anger? (For instance, "My son speaks abrasively because he fears looking weak," or "My daughter is very passive in her anger because she fears that openness will get her into trouble.")

_____

_____

_____

The Many Forms of Defensiveness

Defensiveness, and the fear that drives it, can be displayed in many forms. To get an idea of how this ingredient influences anger in your home, let's look at three separate categories of defensiveness. Do any of these behaviors look familiar to you?

Offensive Defensiveness

Some people display their defensive nature by taking the focus off themselves and keeping it on the ones with whom they are in conflict. Being afraid of the vulnerability that accompanies self-exploration, they prefer to make others uncomfortable:

- "Boomerang" communication, throwing the focus back onto the person making an accusation with a statement like: "What about you?"
- Blaming and accusation
- Being a dictator, allowing very limited choices
- Shifting responsibility, as typified by "I wouldn't have erred if you had done what you were supposed to do"
- Bringing up the past as a way to invalidate the other person
- Keeping score of others' wrongs, which can deflect attention from one's own negative traits
- Using sarcasm to undermine another person's legitimate thoughts
- Being so forceful that no one can register a differing thought or preference

Most people who act offensively do not openly admit that their behavior is a fearful defense of their hidden feelings of weakness. Yet close examination indicates that those who readily act imposing are afraid of letting their hurts be known. The appearance of strength can actually be a cover for great insecurity. The offensive person is insecure because of the fear that he or she will not be heard unless force is used.

Can you think of moments when your defensiveness is portrayed offensively? (For instance, "When my son challenges my judgment, I become defensive and speak in an overpowering fashion," or "My daughter is quietly stubborn, and my abrasive speech is a cover for my fear that she'll immediately dismiss what I have to say.")

_____

_____

_____

How about your children? When do they reveal defensiveness with offensive behavior? (For instance, "My daughter won't listen to me because she's too busy criticizing everything I say," or "My son constantly blames his shortcomings on others.")

_____

_____

_____

_____

The Defense of Denial

Some people add to the atmosphere of conflict by denying that they have problems, even when their problems seem obvious to others. They fear that admitting flaws would make them appear weak, so they defend themselves by denying their flawed humanness:

- Rationalization, meaning problems are whisked away with a presumably air-tight explanation
- "Ain't life grand" syndrome, refusing to discuss anything other than cheery subjects
- Ignoring problems, assuming they will go away if not addressed
- Intellectualizing, turning discussion about feelings into discussion about facts only
- Shallow thinking, refusing to explore the deeper issues of life and relationships
- Being a "know-it-all"
- Playing the "I didn't know any better" card

People who use the defense of denial generally also suppress their anger and lapse early into passive-aggressive communication. They are reluctant to admit what they really feel, which means they often generate frustration in those who try to communicate with them about problematic issues.

Have you ever noticed the presence of this form of defensiveness in your home? How might you as a parent defend yourself by using denial? (For instance, "I can be hard to reach because I don't like to look at the problems that occur in our family," or "I have a habit of justifying my flaws when someone points them out to me.")

_____

_____

_____

What about your children? How do they use denial? (For instance, "My son acts as if everything is terrific even when the rest of us are clearly hurting," or "My daughter won't communicate at all when the subject becomes personal.")

_____

_____

_____

_____

The Defense of Evasiveness

Some people have decided that open discussion of problems creates more problems than it solves. They often refer to distasteful experiences of anger that have produced disastrous results. They live with a fear that further exposure of hurt or needs will bring about the same pain, so they make quite conscious decisions to be evasive when conflict becomes probable:

- Changing the subject to a neutral or friendly topic
- Placating or giving in, as a way to avoid addressing problematic issues

- Being physically unavailable
- Procrastinating, waiting as long as possible to address an emotionally laden subject
- Giving a superficial response
- Maintaining secret lifestyle habits, particularly if the behavior might be questionable
- Staying so busy there is little time to discuss personal matters
- Using a cautious and calculated approach with people

As evasiveness is displayed, it indicates that a low level of trust is influencing the person's relating style. Evasive people are convinced, sometimes rightly so, that too much display of differing ideas will only become problematic. Their exposure to unsafe people has caused them to live with heavy skepticism.

Are you ever evasive with your children? How might this be displayed? (For instance, "I'm known for being a busy worker, and it's often hard to pin me down for personal discussion," or "When my daughter begins arguing with me I'll tell her that I don't want to talk about it, and then I'll leave the room.")

_____

_____

_____

How do your children act evasively? (For instance, "My son is a master at keeping secrets, and I often don't know what he's doing," or "My daughter would rather lie her way out of a problem than discuss it openly.")

_____

_____

_____

All three patterns of defensiveness (being offensive, using denial, and acting evasively) indicate that trust has deteriorated significantly in the home and fear has taken over. As the fear remains unaddressed, anger grows quickly as efforts to address conflict fall apart.

Speaking with Dr. Minirth, Alan realized that defensiveness was pervasive in his communication with Jeron. He would defend himself by becoming so offensive that his son concluded they would never be able to have reasonable conversations regarding their differences. Jeron, however, was less prone toward his father's style of offensiveness; his defensiveness was displayed through denial and evasiveness.

Dr. Minirth explained to Alan: "It's easy to see that there is an anger problem in your home, but to get to the root of your anger both you and Jeron have to identify what it is that you're most afraid of. It's easy to speculate that Jeron is afraid of saying the wrong thing because of the invalidation and punishment it would bring, but let's look at your fear. What fear causes you to become so easily angered?"

This question caught Alan entirely off-guard. He had always seen himself as a highly opinionated man who knew what he believed and what he wanted to accomplish. It didn't seem right to think of himself as fearful. Yet if the doctor was correct in saying that fear is commonly evidenced through defensive behavior, he knew he'd have to plead guilty, because he was certainly defensive.

As Alan pondered the issue of fearfulness, he eventually realized he was afraid of his own son's rejection and the possibility that Jeron would not respect him. Whenever his son would disobey or challenge his assertions, Alan's anger indicated he felt threatened or disrespected ("Hey, I'm threatened by that. It unnerves me that you would think poorly of me. I've got to have your agreement before I can feel secure").

Cultivating Inner Trust

In one of the most beloved verses from Proverbs, we are told: "Trust in the Lord with all your heart and lean not on your own understanding. In all your ways acknowledge him and he will direct your paths" (Proverbs 3:5–6). If we trust in the Lord without leaning on our own understanding, we willingly admit that the natural, sinful manner of responding to life's challenges can quickly get us in trouble. (This includes our reflexive tendency to defend or attack when we feel challenged or threatened.)

We can choose instead to become so familiar with the reasonable teachings of the Lord, and so yielded to his truth, that we consciously opt to put his methods into play instead of our own less-effective methods. This means we are willing to look carefully at our usual responses to determine if they match God's Word. For example, we readily recognize that yelling is inconsistent with the biblical instruction to respond to wrath with a soft response (Proverbs 15:1). Likewise we are reminded that a hot-tempered response only stirs up more trouble (Proverbs 29:22). In addition, we are focused on the truth that love is patient and kind; it lacks arrogance and does not insist on its own way (I Corinthians 13:4–5). Trusting in the Lord is more than just a pleasant-sounding concept. It is nothing short of applied theology in the most personal elements of daily life. It reflects a mind-set that is truly God-directed.

As Alan came to admit the fear associated with his anger, Dr. Minirth challenged him with an alternative: "I'm wondering how you would respond differently to Jeron's abrasive behavior if you chose not to be threatened by it. I understand it's no fun having your son act as if he knows better than you, yet that's nothing to fear. Instead, you can choose to respond with calm confidence because you know that you're using godly wisdom or good logic when you speak words of discipline to him."

Alan replied thoughtfully, "I guess I never thought about it that way, but it makes sense. So how would it work?"

The two men put their heads together and discussed some practical ways Alan could respond with a nonfearful attitude:

- When Jeron questions Alan's unwillingness to give him money for something that seems unnecessary, Alan does not need to defend himself by offensively ripping into his son's "gimme, gimme" attitude. Alan can offer a soft answer to his son's wrath by saying, "Looks like we see the situation differently, but I'm going to stand by my decision."
- Alan has asked Jeron to keep reasonable limits in the use of his cell phone, but Jeron abuses his privileges. When Jeron argues about the restrictions placed on him as a consequence, Alan might lecture him about his insubordinate spirit. Or he can show patience by saying: "I believe the restriction is reasonable. In a week, we can discuss how you can build your phone privileges back to a level we both can live with."

Dr. Minirth explained that there was no reason to defend decisions that need no defense. If Alan was confident that his determinations were reasonable, he could stand firmly on them without blustery fanfare. The more he defended, the more he indicated a feeling of uncertainty, and Jeron would feel empowered to retaliate. Defending himself less would indicate an inner peace and his son would not be so inclined to act as an adversary.

Whether you realize it or not, you send cues to your children, letting them know how fearful or how confident you are. Your aggressive anger is a cue that you are feeling rattled. If you remain consistent in calm assertiveness, the cue is one of confidence.

When you angrily defend your decisions, what cues do your children sense from you? (For instance, "When I yell, it's as though I'm sending an invitation to argue," or "When my son and I debate the merits of my decisions it's as if I'm begging for his approval.")

_____

_____

_____

Likewise, the defensiveness portrayed by your children is their way of sending you cues regarding how they are feeling at the moment. When your children act defensively, what is really being portrayed at that moment? (For instance, "When my daughter rationalizes her irresponsibility, she's indicating that she's afraid I'll invalidate her," or "My son's evasive tactic tells me he's afraid of accountability.")

_____

_____

_____

There is no joy to be found when you are in conflict with your children. Whether the child's anger is openly or passively aggressive, if feels like an affront to you, and naturally you want to protect yourself and your convictions. Since anger can have a legitimate function of self-preservation, it is not wrong for you to assertively stand up for truth. Keep in mind, though, that you do not have to preserve the integrity of your convictions at the child's expense. Even when the child is displaying a caustic or non-cooperative spirit, you can choose to respond with self-confidence leading the way.

Let's examine how your anger can be handled without fearful defense.

Don't Be Threatened by Differentness

No child is ever going to agree with the parents on every subject. In fact, it is predictable that children will second-guess their parents' wisdom many times. One dad joked with his daughter when she turned thirteen: "Honey, now that you're a teenager, you're probably going to discover with each passing year that my IQ will go lower and lower. Around age twenty-five you'll notice that my IQ will slowly begin rising again. In the interim, you'll have to learn how to negotiate the fact that I'm not as smart as you want me to be whenever you and I discuss how things ought to be."

If your children indicate that they think your ideas are off, don't be shocked. Beginning in the preteen years, they want to spread their wings and fly . . . and they may often assume that they need no input from you. As they progress in age, they will want to try out different priorities or skills, because it is part of learning who they are. Just as adults may stumble in trying to incorporate new priorities, your kids will too. Rather than being threatened by their desire to take paths different from yours, work with them.

Consider what differences threaten you most when your children are unruly. What are some of the common issues? (For instance, "I am greatly bothered when my son seems interested in the drug crowd or those who like alcohol," or "I am bothered when it is obvious that my daughter is just humoring me.")

_____

_____

_____

You may not like the differences between you and your children, and they may exhibit immaturity in communicating their preferences, but the fact that you do not agree is not odd. Would you be willing to factor in large doses of differentness?

"So let me get this straight," said Alan. "You're suggesting that I should just shrug it off when Jeron disagrees with me, even if he's way off-base in his thinking?"

"I'm not suggesting you should hold any less firmly to your convictions," was the doctor's reply. "I'm saying that young people like to think they know best, so when you get an adversarial response there's no reason to be blown away."

Most of us admit that we enjoy uniqueness if it involves a pleasant or interesting subject. (For instance, we can make room for unique choices in decorating, or music, or how to spend free time.) Maturity is on display if you can allow uniqueness even though you dislike the other's perspective or how it is communicated.

Let Understanding Be Your Primary Goal

Once you set aside the demand that your children must think and react exactly as you would like, you are poised to insert healthy ingredients into the exchange. Rather than engaging in defensive posturing, you can derail the argumentative process by displaying an understanding spirit. (This is consistent with the soft answer to wrath mentioned in the Proverbs.)

It is relatively easy to be understanding when the atmosphere is pleasant and agreeable. When you and your children are in harmony, you are more inclined to speak words of support and hear what the other person has to say. A nonfearful person is able to display understanding even if the atmosphere is unfriendly. Efforts to know the reasoning or motive behind a person's words can still be made even if those words sting.

Alan was able to decrease the anger level with Jeron on one occasion when his son was in a defiant mood. He had expressed reservations about plans Jeron had to attend a party after a Friday night basketball game. Specifically, Alan was suspicious that the host of the party might be supplying beer for the teenagers. As they spoke, Jeron shot back at his dad, "You don't even know what you're talking about. Yeah, my friend got caught drinking a couple of weeks ago, but his parents came down on him hard. There's no way he's going to do something stupid like that again tonight."

Normally Alan would have responded defensively to his son's challenging tone of voice, but he remembered his discussions about fear and confidence. This time he responded by determining not to defend. "Sounds like your buddy may be wising up. Fill me in on the latest. What do you and your buddies think about underage drinking?"

This approach was definitely not what Jeron expected, but he liked it. His voice became less agitated and he and his dad had a ten-minute talk about the seriousness of the matter. Alan was satisfied that his son was being honest with him, and Jeron was relieved that his dad would listen.

Alan's nondefensive reaction began with "I'm not afraid to discuss the subject of drinking with my son; I'd like to know more about his feelings on the subject." By being understanding, he was able to move beyond his own defensive thinking and become an ally with his son, who was facing a crucial issue that required adult guidance. Afterward, they had their own long discussion about the pros and cons of alcohol use, and Alan was able to make his point without sounding preachy.

Think about the times when it is unnatural to demonstrate understanding. Can you relate to any of these tensions?

- Your child listens to your directives for the specific purpose of telling you why your ideas are wrong
- As you attempt to guide your child toward responsible tasks, you hear excuses about why he or she shouldn't have to do what you say
- In the effort to get your child to cooperate, you encounter a grumbling, complaining spirit
- Your child deliberately gives you the silent treatment as you try to talk about something important
- During a discussion, you know your child is lying

It requires great patience on your part to show understanding in such adverse circumstances, but it can be done. Remember, although you may not like their responses, you need not be afraid of them. Clearly, when children are evasive or adversarial, they are hurting. Are you will-

ing to be less imposing during those moments as you opt for a prob-
ing, understanding response?

Think carefully. Why does your child act defensively or respond dis-
agreeably? (For instance, "My daughter likes to do things on her own
timetable, with no intrusion from me," or "My son has such a need for
peer acceptance that he's capable of making poor judgments in how he
conducts his social life.")

_____

_____

_____

Even if you disagree with your child's feelings or perceived needs, are
you willing to communicate an understanding of your child in those
moments? How would such willingness affect your communication style?
(For instance, "I'd cease lecturing, and I would gather input from my
son regarding his ideas," or "I'd let my daughter know that I respect her
preferences and desires, even as I work to bring harmony to the ways
we coordinate family life.")

_____

_____

_____

What effect can your understanding approach have on your child's anger?
(For instance, "If I choose not to argue, he'll be less pushy," or "My willingness to be open-minded might soften my daughter's stubbornness.")

_____

_____

_____

Modify Your Leadership Style

If fearful defensiveness is part of your pattern with your children, you cease
displaying leadership as you allow yourself to be swept into the undertow
of insecure exchanges. With no leadership in a time of disagreement,

the possibility of successfully managing anger diminishes greatly. By definition, leaders do not merely react to circumstances; they initiate. This means that you need not allow your young to set your pace; you can establish your own pace. You can be objective when they are subjective. You can be accepting when they are rejecting. You can be confident when they have no confidence in you. You can be calm when they are high-strung.

Alan's greatest challenge was to remain aware of his choices in the moments when he and Jeron disagreed. He came to realize that defending himself was a choice, as was yelling, pleading, threatening, and insulting. They were lousy choices, to be sure, but they were choices nonetheless. As he acknowledged that his ultimate goal was to help defuse Jeron's anger while teaching him solid values, Alan concluded that nondefensive responses were a choice that held great promise.

Dr. Minirth challenged him: "Alan, you initially sought treatment to lessen your mood swings, and then you specified that you did not want your son to follow the same path. To accomplish your goal, you'll need to establish a course of clean emotional management so you can be the model for Jeron to follow. That means you'll need to rise above his quibbling ways and show him by example what respectful communication looks like. Also, let's recognize that your efforts will require years, not days, of due diligence."

Since defensiveness indicates fear, and since leadership is anchored in confidence, not fear, Alan had to predetermine how he could lay aside his defenses if Jeron "invited" him into a nonproductive exchange. He thought deeply about the kind of family leader he wanted to be. In his contemplative moments, he admitted he wanted to be firm and principled, yet he wanted that to be accompanied by such qualities as respectfulness, kindness, and encouragement. Such an approach to leadership would be quickly derailed if he were merely a defensive reactor to his son's immature ramblings. As the leader, he could choose to show maturity amid conflict.

How do you envision yourself as a leader in your relationship with your children? (For instance, "I want to show my son how objectivity can be used as we explore solutions for our problems," or "I want my daughter to see in me that it is possible to remain respectful even in disagreement.")

_____

_____

_____

How does your defensive behavior spoil your leadership ability? (For instance, "When I join with my son in the accusing game, it makes me look petty or mean-spirited," or "The more I try to justify my choices, the more my daughter turns a deaf ear to me.")

_____

_____

_____

How might a calm, confident tone of voice increase your leadership status? (For instance, "I'd be displaying the very characteristic that I'm asking my kids to have," or "I'd be sane in the midst of volatility.")

_____

_____

_____

Let Correctness Become a Secondary Issue

When parents enter into a defensive-offensive battle with their children, they usually dig themselves deep into a hole of anger because they are so intent on being correct that they lose emotional composure. In the struggle, they snap emotionally as it becomes apparent that the child is trying to invalidate parental authority, and trying to inject a better idea. In the defensive posture, the parental goal is to communicate: "I'll show you how right I am!" The message is not well received by the child because it is so condescending.

Correctness is good, but it is not the ultimate good. Perhaps you have heard the old saying, "People don't care about how much you know until they know how much you care." While in the argumentative mode, you may be emphasizing the facts of right versus wrong, but you should realize that the child is responding to your emotionality more than to the facts. Your emphasis on patience, composure, and tolerance is therefore highly influential as you attempt to gain your child's cooperation.

If you focus less on correctness and more on emotional composure, how will your defensiveness decrease? (For instance, "I'll be more able to demonstrate empathy even if I disagree with my kids," or "I won't go into a repetitive communication cycle, which tends to increase my anger.")

_____

_____

_____

_____

It is never pleasant to receive back talk, sarcasm, or invalidation from your child. Yet as unpleasant as it can be, you need not fear it. Recognize that as children attempt to develop independent thinking, they take offense at parental guidance because they want to believe they know what is best. That is not a bad desire. Even as you talk with them about how to align their independent desires with the needs of the family, respect can be maintained. Assume that there will be numerous incidents when the child disagrees, and don't live in dread that you cannot handle such a possibility. As you keep your focus on your goals of love, in time they can appreciate the correctness that is also part of your message.

For Family Discussion

1. Have each family member identify the times when he or she is most likely to be defensive. What are you threatened by at that moment?

2. Allow each person to describe how he or she sees other family members acting defensively. How does this increase the problem of anger in the home?

3. When do you try to protect yourself by focusing instead on the faults of others? Why do you feel the need to protect yourself this way?

4. When you trust that you are on the right track with your life, you are much less likely to be defensive if others find fault in you. How does inner confidence decrease your tendency to be defensive?

5. Openness is an essential ingredient for families who are trying to grow together. How can you add to a positive family atmosphere by demonstrating an open spirit even though others have different opinions?

6. By dropping your need for defensiveness, you indicate that you do not always have to be right. What positive things could happen in your family if each of you is less worried about being right?

7. Have each person identify how he or she contributes to the others' defensive responses. What are you willing to change to help your family members feel less defensive in your presence?

For Further Reflection

II Timothy 1:7 states: "For God has not given us a spirit of timidity, but of power and love and discipline."

1. If timidity or fear is not from God, where does it come from? How can your anger be understood as an indicator of fear? How can your child's anger be understood as an indicator of fear?

2. When you let defensiveness creep into your moments of conflict, what exactly are you defending? Why? When your children respond defensively, what are they defending? Why?

Psalm 56:3–4 renders the words of confidence: "When I am afraid, I will put my trust in Thee. . . . What can mere men do to me?"

3. There is no need to remain threatened when you are trusting in God's guidance. As a parent, what does it mean to put your trust in God? How will this trust have an impact on your use of anger when your children act adversarially?

4. Knowing that your children's anger can be anchored in fear of you, how might you respond so as to minimize that fear? What signals from you are your kids looking for that indicate you are trustworthy?

Proverbs 13:1 tells us: "A wise son accepts his father's discipline, but a scoffer does not listen to rebuke."

5. To teach listening skills to your children, you must first model them. What makes listening a difficult skill? When a child is speaking words of anger, what options do you have as you try to establish yourself as a good listener?

6. Listening helps soften your children's defenses. What do you suppose your children want you to hear when they feel angry? Rather than engaging in a debate at that moment, how can you defuse the atmosphere of fear?

9

ESTABLISHING BOUNDARIES

Step 9: *Respect the fact that each family member is responsible for his or her choices.*

To manage your anger successfully and guide your children through anger wisely, you cannot allow your mood to become so enmeshed with theirs that you lose sight of what you wish to accomplish as a parent. Because it is so predictable that children can and will mismanage anger, it is essential for parents to operate on a separate level. This means that you understand the value of relationship boundaries.

Parents naturally want their offspring to succeed in life. Even if there is a history of great contention, most still care very deeply about the well-being of their children, which can be both positive and negative. It is positive, of course, for parents to remain heavily invested in their children because it stimulates bonding and persistence. It can be negative, though, if parents become so concerned for their children that they allow the children to determine the emotional stability of the home. Too many moms and dads experience erratic emotions because they have not learned to think of themselves as separate and distinct from their children. Having relationship boundaries means everyone determining for themselves who they will be and how they will conduct their lives. The lack of well-defined boundaries ensures anger.

Marilyn had three sons, ages fifteen, thirteen, and ten, and she described her home as "a regular madhouse." She sought counseling because of depression and anxiety symptoms, but it was not long before she shared with Dr. Carter how exasperated she felt because of her parenting challenges. "I feel like a failure as a mother," she said through tears. "My oldest son, Preston, rules over the other two like a tyrant. He's bossy and mean, and he keeps his brothers on edge because they never know when he's going to bust loose with a temper tantrum. It often leads to shoving and shouting. I'll get pulled into the middle and before you know it, I'm shouting too, and the whole family just seems to fall apart."

Making matters more difficult for Marilyn, her husband traveled frequently, which left her feeling she could never afford to let down her guard. She regularly felt outnumbered as her efforts to bring sanity to the boys' argumentative chaos easily got out of hand. When Dr. Carter first suggested that she could learn to manage her anger successfully, she looked defeated as she replied, "When I hear you say that, I wonder if maybe I'm just too far gone. I'm not sure we can change at this point."

When we talk with parents like Marilyn, we never assume that change is quick and simple. It might be relatively easy to prescribe changes in thinking and behavioral patterns, but we recognize that the problems feeding anger did not arise suddenly, nor do they go away suddenly. Yet because we believe in the resilience of the human spirit, we know that old patterns can be understood and then exchanged for better ways. This belief guides us as we help parents recognize the need to establish successful boundaries with their children.

What Are Boundaries?

Let's clarify what we mean when we refer to the need for boundaries. Just as physical property has boundary lines, the same can be said for personalities. For instance, you know clearly where the boundary line is between your home and your neighbor's lot. You can also recognize the common sense of choosing to let your neighbor tend to the upkeep of his or her property, just as you will tend to your own. Each individual likewise can be taught to make choices regarding his or her own emotions, with the realization that it is not the responsibility of others to do so.

Let's examine four defining ingredients inherent in relationship boundaries.

Recognizing the Uniqueness of Each Personality

Do you remember cutting out paper snowflakes when you were an elementary schoolchild? Once all of you had cut your snowflakes, the teacher would remark, "No two snowflakes ever look alike." The same can be said of personalities. No two people have the exact set of ingredients, nor do any two people have the same purpose or mission in life. DNA research has provided fascinating evidence that each individual is uniquely created; no one can be expected to have exactly the same tendencies as anyone else.

When parents become angry with children, and children become angry with parents, what is it that they each want in their frustration? Sameness of thought! The parents want the children to use the same logic they hold, and the children want the parents to view the world just as they do. Far from being celebrated, uniqueness or differentness is greatly scorned. Through anger, the message is sent, "It's not OK for you to be you. You ought to be the person I want you to be!" This thought represents confusion with boundaries.

In what circumstances do you feel that the uniqueness of the individuals in your family is scorned? (For instance, "My son has a very strong personality, but I'd rather he have a milder temperament like me," or "I've got strong views about my religion, and I hate it when my daughter displays attitudes inconsistent with my beliefs.")

_____

_____

_____

It is natural for parents to want their children to have similar values or cooperative ways of managing conflicts. But in the zeal to create cooperation, we often overlook the truth that others can only be what they are, and not a replica of what you desire. I Corinthians 12:12 reminds us that the Holy Spirit distributes "to each one individually as he wills." This reflects the truth that God specifically creates each person with separate tendencies. It also implies that those seeking to be mature in their relationships learn to work with others, recognizing fully that sameness of thought and behavior does not always happen.

For instance, Marilyn's oldest son, Preston, was strong-willed, while she was generally mild-mannered. Much of her anger toward him stemmed from her desire for Preston to be like her: less bossy and more tolerant. But he was not going to be that way. Preston was uniquely Preston, and Marilyn was going to have great frustration so long as she wished she could somehow make him become something he would not be. Her desire to have more sameness between herself and her son caused her to overlook the truth that Preston's personality could be an asset. It caused him to be stubborn, but he was also decisive, and that was good. Her anger would be triggered over and over so long as she could not recognize that his personality was a unique blend of traits that set him apart from other individuals.

Think of the many ways your kids display traits unique to them. How can you show acceptance for that uniqueness, even though it may be outside the box? (For instance, "My son is more strong-willed than me, but that can be good because it also means he's a natural leader," or "My daughter is slow to do things, but she's also more tolerant than a lot of other kids.")

_____

_____

_____

Accepting and Encouraging Individual Responsibility

Since each person "owns" a unique set of traits and preferences, it stands to reason that each is required to do the best with what he or she has. When parents let anger get the best of them, it is almost always because they are working too hard to take responsibility for their children's issues.

It is as if they wish they could enter the child's mind for the purpose of making the child's choices on his or her behalf.

The fourth chapter of Proverbs focuses on the words of a kind father instructing his children to follow the steps of wisdom. As you read the words of this great chapter, you sense how lovingly they must have been spoken originally. The father tells his children not to forsake God's law, to love wisdom, to honor understanding, and to stay away from wickedness. Clearly the father was directive in his teaching style, yet as you read his words you get the distinct impression that he recognizes "it is ultimately up to you if you will receive my words." This is how it works with relationship boundaries. Teach, and then stand back and allow the child to absorb.

Whenever Preston tormented one of his younger brothers, Marilyn would instantly think, *I've got to make him realize that he can't act that way. He's got to learn to treat his brothers respectfully.* Though her sentiment was noble, she made an error in thinking that she could take over her son's reasoning, which she could not. She *could* teach him to take responsibility for his choices. For instance, in her agitated state of anger she might say, "What do I have to do to make you realize that you cannot continue to behave as you do?" This would represent confusion about boundaries because it implied she was taking responsibility for how he thought. As an alternative, she could recognize his uniqueness and say: "Preston, when I get angry I've decided that it's still best to treat people with respect, and that's a choice that would be wise for you as well. Nonetheless, this is your life, so you'll be the one making your own choices. Understand that when you choose to berate your brother, it comes with the consequence of isolation and no social activities for the weekend. I'll let you decide if that's what you want."

Trying to angrily force solutions is not as effective as giving the child the responsibility to sift out his or her own thoughts about consequences. By staying out of the anger trap, you let the child realize that he or she, and not you, ultimately gets to choose what happens.

How do you work too hard to take responsibility for your child's choices? (For instance, "I'm constantly pleading with my daughter to become better organized," or "When my son gives me rude responses I'll argue with him about the way he ought to treat me, but he never relents.")

_____

_____

_____

You can encourage your children to take more personal responsibility by persuading less and instead letting them ponder their own thoughts about the merits of the consequences their choices bring.

Defining What You Are and What You Are Not

No parent specifically wants to be regarded as angry, blustery, or harsh. Yet in the heat of conflict with their children, they can act in opposition to what they believe to be best. This behavior is another example of boundary confusion. Rather than living according to a well-conceived plan, parents allow their emotional response to be determined by the children.

Think of this analogy. Let's suppose it's Saturday morning at your home and you recognize that some major housecleaning is in order. So you say, "I'm going to have to check with my next-door neighbor to see what she thinks about my cleaning house. I wonder if she'll tell me that I ought to vacuum the floors, or I wonder if she thinks it would be a good idea if I clean the dishes in my sink." That's absurd! It's not your neighbor's responsibility to define for you how you should proceed with your housecleaning chores. It's your home, so decide for yourself how you will proceed.

In the same vein, it is not your children who will define for you how you should proceed in disciplining circumstances. It's your personality, so you are the one who determines what you will do with it.

When is it most necessary for you to establish your own definition regarding your behavior and priorities? (For instance, "If my son has an I-don't-care-attitude, I need to remain respectful in the way I speak to him," or "If my daughter makes it clear that she's ready and willing to argue with me, I don't need to join in her combative spirit.")

_____

_____

_____

You can communicate most effectively to your children if your own life skills are anchored in stable emotions. When your life consists of erratic emotions, you teach your children to do the same. When your life consists of a well-defined plan accompanied by patience and respect, you teach them that they too can make such a plan regarding how they choose to treat others.

Recognizing the Reality of Limits

In the physical world, boundary lines serve to remind you that you cannot have it all. For instance, reaching into your pantry you can select whatever food items you want, and you can eat them right there. When you go to the grocery store, you are more limited, in the sense that you cannot just grab food and eat it as you might please. Once you leave your personal property, you accept limits regarding how you behave elsewhere.

Families consist of limits, too. Dad is limited in what he can make Mom do, and vice versa. Mom and Dad are limited in what they can get their children to do. Each unique personality is a separate entity unto itself; a healthy family makes room for that reality.

In Marilyn's home, it was clear that Preston had not yet come to terms with the limits that existed between him and his younger brothers. He generally acted as if he should have unlimited access to their lives by telling them what to do and by choosing to ignore the rules that pertained to each of the sons. As Marilyn responded to Preston's undesirable behavior, she too would ignore the reality of her limits. She would plead persuasively with him as if she could somehow get inside his mind to make him think as she wanted him to think. Of course, Preston repeatedly proved how limited she was by not allowing her to rearrange his priorities, yet in one incident after another Marilyn would ignore her limits as she repeatedly tried to persuade him in some way that he would ignore.

When is it clear that you ignore your limits as you try to force your agenda onto your kids? (For instance, "When my kids argue with each other, I become highly frustrated because it's obvious that they are forgetting the many discussions I've had with them regarding the need for harmony," or "Over and over I plead with my daughter to understand the value of personal discipline, but she just ignores me.")

_____

_____

_____

As a parent, you are limited in your ability to make your child prioritize life as you wish. You can speak with conviction and apply consequences repeatedly; such approaches are good and necessary. Don't be surprised, however, if your children through their behavior continue to exercise independence contrarily. Consequences can be continued, but you may be forced to accept that there is a boundary between your mind and your child's mind that cannot be crossed.

Characteristics of Boundary Confusion

When we discuss boundaries with parents like Marilyn, we often hear words of agreement. Then we hear that fateful word _but_. Marilyn spoke with Dr. Carter about her struggles with Preston. "I know I need to accept that he thinks differently from me and that his personality causes him to have different preferences, _but_ I've got to figure out a way to make him understand that he can't continue being a terror at home."

At first glance, Marilyn's statement might seem reasonable. Notice, though, where her primary focus lay. She wanted to rearrange his thinking. Dr. Carter explained to her, "Your desires are very reasonable; I'd like to help you redirect your focus. Preston has repeatedly refused to let down his walls of defense when you appeal to his logic, and each time you try to break down his boundaries by arguing, he proves again that he won't let you in. Rather than trying to force what you cannot change, stand on what you can control."

As an example, Preston had a way of making mealtime miserable for the rest of the family. So instead of pleading with him about his attitude Marilyn explained to her son: "For the next week the rest of us will eat together, and then once we finish, you can have your dinner.

That's the way it will work if you choose to argue when you're with all of us." Likewise, whenever Preston dominated the computer and would not allow his brother to use it for a homework assignment, Marilyn explained, "If you choose not to be cooperative, you choose to stay in on Friday night. I'm willing to work with you to have the lifestyle you want, and you'll find that the effort will be much smoother if you choose to work with me, too."

Marilyn was realizing she could not force Preston to have the very disposition she wished him to have, but she could establish boundaries to assist him in the process of rethinking his behaviors. It was hard to give up on the notion that she could force him to be the son she dreamed of, but with the doctor's help she was realizing that her role was to establish reasonable rules and firm consequences, while Preston's job was to determine how he would adjust to her common sense.

To get an idea of whether you are displaying boundaries confusion as you discipline your children, look over this list of traits. Place a check next to the ones you use fairly frequently.

_____ Disregard for the feelings of others
_____ Placing such a heavy focus on your own agenda that you are unable to accept the other person's needs
_____ Displaying poor listening skills
_____ Being defensive to the point of being close-minded
_____ Difficulty admitting errors or mistakes
_____ Overuse of criticism and suggestions
_____ Interrupting during a conversation
_____ Letting your anger take you toward rude behavior
_____ Having a "do it my way" mentality
_____ Using guilt as a means of creating motivation in the other person

As you use traits like these, you imply being so fixed on your own agenda that you make little room for the feelings and needs of others. You probably have great difficulty accepting your inability to make the other person think exactly as you do.

How do you most commonly show you are struggling to accept the reality that your child has boundaries that differ from yours? (For instance,

"I cannot accept the fact that my daughter doesn't want to learn to play the piano," or "I'm constantly using guilt trips to force my son to appreciate all that I do for him.")

_____

_____

_____

Now go back through the list and place your children's initials next to the traits that indicate their difficulty in respecting boundaries. Try to become aware of how they show that they have not yet learned they are limited in their ability to make you think as they want you to think.

How do your kids illustrate that they have not yet learned good boundaries with you? (For instance, "My son acts as if I should agree that it's OK for him to maintain his bad habits," or "My daughter tries to make me feel guilty when I hold firmly to consequences.")

_____

_____

_____

Are you willing _not_ to become pulled into their boundary confusion? This requires you to sustain firmness regarding your legitimate needs and convictions without trying to mold and shape your child into the form that pleases you.

Marilyn once asked Dr. Carter, "But isn't it my job as a parent to make sure my children have the right values, and that those values are reflected in their behavior?"

He replied, "Your question reflects a fair desire, but even as we examine the answer, let's hold on to the reality that your children's personalities do not belong to you. It _is_ your job to teach good values, and this is done via oral explanation as well as through your life's example. It _is_ your job to also create a system of rewards and consequences to let them know that cooperation brings positive results and lack of cooperation brings negative results."

Rounding out his response, he explained to Marilyn, "It is *not* your job to make them like everything you say. Likewise, it is *not* your job to force them to have a good attitude even as you seek to gain behavioral compliance. *Do* hold firmly to your convictions. *Do* stick with reasonable consequences. Respect them even if they do not respect you. In the long run, as you allow them room to consider your leadership style, your fair-mindedness and your even temperament can prevail in a way that intrusive words never will."

Healthy Anger and Boundaries

Let's take a look at some specific ways you can manage anger cleanly even as you recognize the limits of your influence. Keep in mind that as you maintain consistency in boundaries, your children will eventually be more open during the times you wish to talk with them about their use of anger.

Don't "Sell" the Legitimacy of Your Convictions

One of the greatest mistakes parents can make is to work too hard in selling their children on the viability of their ideas. Do you ever fall into this trap? Many parents seem genuinely amazed when their instructions to their children are met by resistance and rebuttal. Even so, this behavior is found in virtually every family, so drop your shock!

When you give guidance to your kids, they are often predisposed to test your resolve. They are curious to know just how serious you are about holding firmly to your convictions. This explains why they verbally challenge you or dawdle in their response. If you respond to their challenges with persuasion, they might say to themselves: "Well, well. You certainly are working hard to convince me of your correctness. I think I may just push back a little more." This pushing back may consist of more argument or passivity. At this juncture, you can choose to play the game or opt out.

When your kids choose to challenge your guidance, how do you keep the unhealthy atmosphere alive through a persuasive response? (For instance, "I'll ask questions like 'What's wrong with you?' or 'Why do we always have to turn things into a struggle?'" or "I'll try to convince my son of the illogic in his thinking.")

_____

_____

_____

Keeping in mind that good boundaries include a willingness to let the other person define his or her own direction, you can opt out of the persuasive approach by giving the children room to choose for themselves how they will proceed. As an example, Preston developed a habit of not doing all his homework, though he would tell his mother that all was fine with school. When he received a poor report card, it was obvious to her that he had been dishonest with her.

"My first impulse," she told the doctor, "was to yell at him for lying and to give him a lecture about the necessity of preparing himself for college. Then I realized how intrusive I can be when I try to sell him on the correctness of my ideas. So instead, I looked at Preston and told him that ultimately he would be the one to live with the results of his poor efforts, not me. As a consequence for his laziness and his lying, I grounded him *one more time* from the after-school activities he likes. I told him that I'd still give consequences when he directly defied house rules, but I was not going to beg him to be a good student. I mentioned to him that I can only go so far in exposing him to good values, and the rest is up to him."

It can be hard for parents like Marilyn to cease lecturing or pleading when their children's future is hanging in the balance. Nevertheless, she correctly determined that she could explain her desires and establish consequences, and then Preston still had the responsibility to choose for himself where he would go from there. As the months passed, she witnessed how her son still struggled to be the responsible teenager she wanted him to be, yet as she removed herself from fruitless debate he had less reason to act rebelliously toward her. Their relationship slowly improved, and her influence slowly increased.

How will your anger be affected if you choose to persuade less and let your children come to terms with consequences on their own? (For instance, "The number of arguments with my son would definitely decrease because I'd be less insistent, even with my firmness," or "Once I explain my boundaries to my daughter, I would not take it upon myself to make her like my ideas, which means I'd be less pushy.")

_____

_____

_____

How do you suppose your kids' anger will be affected if you hold to your convictions without having to get immediate approval from them? (For instance, "My daughter would still be ticked off when I give consequences, but her anger would abate sooner once it becomes obvious that I'll cease from pleading," or "My son gets most angry at my insistent nature, so if I choose to be more matter-of-fact, he'll be less inclined to attack.")

_____

_____

_____

Be a Teacher During Opportune Moments

Choosing not to sell your ideas to your kids does not imply that you should cease speaking at all about your beliefs. In your effort to apply assertiveness, you can still inject your beliefs instructively. Hebrews 12:8–10 reminds us that God's love is known by the way he chastens us, just as a father chastens his young. Loving parents _will_ be directive in prompting their young to do good, and the key to their teaching success is lack of harshness. Whereas boundary confusion often leads to a forceful and intrusive communication of beliefs, it does not have to be so.

Dr. Carter coached Marilyn regarding a way to positively influence Preston as she responded to his problematic anger. "When your family is in the heat of tension, that's not the time to speak deeply about your convictions. When you're no longer in the damage-control mode, and there's a lull in tension, that would be a better time to talk calmly with

Preston about your aspirations for him. Without pleading, you can let him know how you place a high premium on kindness, cooperation, and respect. You can even discuss healthy alternatives for how he can respond when his frustrations begin to rise."

Marilyn was frustrated because her many run-ins with Preston resulted in a crushed spirit: "Whenever I try to talk like that with him, he just crosses his arms and stares straight ahead. I don't do a very good job of convincing him of any new ideas."

"Your job is not to convince, but to lovingly convey truth and good values," replied the doctor. "I've spoken with adults in their twenties and thirties who had a lot of conflict with their parents during the teen years, and I've learned that years can go by before some people will finally incorporate what their parents were saying. Those who eventually come around to their parents' values remark that it was their parents' persistence and patience that made the difference."

What message do you most desire to communicate to your children? (For instance, "I want my daughter to understand how her moods could be more steady if she learned to be more secure," or "I wish I could get my son to understand the virtue of gentleness.")

Be willing to lovingly express your convictions to your children even if it appears you are not making an impact at all. The combination of caring words and a steady lifestyle can eventually cause your children to rethink their priorities. Dr. Carter explained to Marilyn: "Right now it seems that Preston has a strong commitment to his anger, and it frustrates you to admit that you're limited in your influence due to the differences that exist between you and him. We both agree, though, that he needs to hear the message you have to offer. As you talk regularly about good values and as you display an even temperament to him, you may be reaching into the core of his thoughts more than he's letting you know."

It can be difficult to let time pass allowing your children to absorb your thoughts at their pace, not yours. It may be years before you see the ultimate results that will satisfy you. But as your children are allowed to incorporate your truth without it being forcefully fed, their eventual willingness to live with your values increases.

How will your approach to conflict management change if you view yourself as a teacher who refuses to force-feed your values? (For instance, "If my son and I clash, I'll still let him know my preferences, but I'll be much less coercive," or "I'll remember that it takes time for my daughter to develop the maturity to appreciate my words, so I'll speak with more calmness and accept her as she is.")

_____

_____

_____

Have Empathy, Even If You Don't Agree

When parents and children display a disregard for each other's boundaries, there is almost always a war of wills being waged. Each is so intent on gaining control of the other's thoughts and priorities that little true understanding occurs. Though it is reasonable to want your kids to hear your perspectives, you are likely to sabotage your goal if your method is primarily intrusive.

Perhaps you are aware of the old proverb, "To have a friend you must be a friend." A corollary to this saying might be, "To be understood, you must show understanding." Instead of crossing your children's boundaries in an effort to force understanding, you are more apt to achieve your goal if you illustrate good understanding. Your behaviors and your demeanor communicate much more powerfully than your agitated words.

Marilyn's greatest struggle in her effort to respond correctly to Preston's anger was in modeling the behavior she wanted him to adopt. "His personality can be so overwhelming that I get pulled into his mood of pessimism," she lamented. As she worked with the doctor to learn how to respect her son's boundaries and stay within her own plan, she was challenged to defuse his anger by making objective, understanding remarks:

• When Preston flew into a rage because of a dispute with one of his brothers, she isolated him in his bedroom for some cooling-off time. Later, sitting on the edge of his bed, she remarked: "I'm very aware that it's hard to be patient when a younger child can't comprehend why you have the priorities you do. Patience on your part would serve you well, although I realize you want quick results."

• When Preston confessed to trying cigarettes with a friend, Marilyn was predictably disappointed. Instead of lecturing him about the perils of tobacco use, she tried a less intrusive approach: "Curiosity is a common quality in young people, so I'm not shocked to know that it caught up with you. You know I don't want you to smoke, and we'll need to find an appropriate consequence to help you see the seriousness of my concerns. Right now, though, I'm more interested in hearing about how the temptation got the best of you."

By taking the time to slow down and summarize what Preston was feeling, she was able to stay out of the anger trap while also showing respect for his feelings, even though she disagreed with those feelings. Dr. Carter summarized the benefits of this approach by saying: "I hope that an empathic spirit can accomplish two things. First, you will throw much less fuel onto his anger, which keeps the combustion from being too powerful. Second, you can pave the way for Preston to hear more of what you have to say because your willingness to consider his perspective can soften his contrariness."

When your children are pushy with their moods, what is it that they wish you could understand? (For instance, "My daughter's argumentative behavior is usually an indication that she wants freedom," or "My son wishes I could understand how important it is to feel respected.")

_____

_____

_____

Even if you disagree with your child's feelings, you can still be a positive influence by taking the time to hear and understand. How can your relationship with your kids improve if you make this a high priority? (For instance, "I'd show that I'm willing to let my son have some uniqueness in his way of thought," or "As I empathize with my daughter she'd feel more respected, and in time she could show respect in return.")

_____

_____

_____

_____

The willingness to acknowledge separate boundaries requires self-restraint, and it also requires parents to accept the reality that their children are separate entities. To further aid you in defusing the anger in your home, in the next chapter we look at how to dispel some common myths that often plague conflicted families.

For Family Discussion

1. Put the focus on each family member one at a time. Identify at least three things that stand out about that person as unique. When you finish, have each person share why it is good to celebrate unique qualities.

2. Now go around the room and have each person identify experiences in which he or she felt it was deemed not OK to be unique. Discuss how these incidents could have been handled more positively.

3. Having good boundaries means that each person is expected to be responsible for his or her life. Focus on each person and have the family identify how they would like that person to take greater responsibility for his or her circumstances. What should happen when that individual chooses not to be responsible?

4. Boundary confusion can happen when an individual does not have well-defined limits. What are some of the limits that should be maintained by each family member (for example, regarding money, time management, giving advice, and so on)?

5. With good boundaries, you can choose to show understanding toward one another even if you do not agree. Have each person give at least two examples of situations where it would be good to feel more understood and accepted.

For Further Reflection

Romans 12:4 states that "just as we have many members in one body and all the members do not have the same function, so we who are many, are one body in Christ, and individually members of one another."

1. God never intended any group of individuals to have so many overlapping traits that uniqueness is lost. How is family unity enhanced when we make allowances for differences in feelings, needs, and perceptions? How do the members of your family differ?

2. To have a good sense of boundaries within the home, it is necessary to allow each person to feel free to be himself or herself. How can this best be accomplished?

3. Coordination is necessary among family members. How can family members develop a sense of coordination without stripping one another of individual uniqueness? What is it about conflict that makes this task unnatural?

4. Think about the different qualities that are a part of assertive anger and aggressive anger. How do aggressive people show disrespect for boundaries? How do assertive people maintain an appreciation for boundaries?

Ephesians 4:29 indicates that it is not wise to speak unwholesome words; rather, we must be committed to words of edification.

5. When relationship boundaries are violated, it is common for unwholesome words to be spoken. Why does this happen? What internal struggles might we expect to find in someone who is pushy or unwholesome?

6. How can a parent remain true to convictions and discipline while also maintaining a spirit of edification?

7. How can you help your children recognize that you are willing to allow them to think for themselves even as you ask them to be considerate of the needs of the overall family?

10

MYTHS THAT PERPETUATE ANGER

Step 10: *Identify the false assumptions that feed your anger, and let truth guide your decisions in discipline.*

In each of the cases we have discussed so far, the parents did not have problems with anger because of mean or nasty intentions toward their children. Quite the contrary, these parents are driven by lofty ideals about how family life should proceed. Like virtually all parents, when their kids entered the world they projected into the future and envisioned a satisfying relationship with their sons and daughters.

Pause for just a moment to recall what you thought and felt when each of your children was born. Like most of us, you probably have quite positive memories, and you can easily recollect thinking how you wanted to have the best of attachments with your young ones as the years unfolded.

What ideals did you cling to at the beginning of your relationship with your children? (For instance, "I can remember smiling often as I envisioned my daughter and me having warm, heart-to-heart talks as she aged," or "I remember thinking how pleased I was to have a boy that I could guide and nurture all the way into manhood.")

It is good to have ideals to guide our relations with our children. They give us something to look forward to, and they motivate us to be the best we can be. Recall, for instance, how Alan sought out counseling with his sixteen-year-old son, Jeron, and how Dr. Minirth coached him to react less defensively toward his son. In the very beginning of their relationship, Alan did not envision himself being the tense or uptight dad that he became. Instead, he envisioned how he and Jeron would enjoy traditional father-and-son interests, and how they would be able to communicate freely about a range of subjects.

Somewhere along the way, as Jeron aged, life took some sharp turns in a direction Alan had not anticipated. It turned out that they did not have many similar interests; Jeron did not warmly respond to his dad's efforts to bond. Instead of the man-to-man discussions Alan once envisioned, their communication more closely resembled the style of prosecuting and defense attorneys. Virtually every time their communication went in the wrong direction, Alan would cringe as he thought, *It's not supposed to be like this. I never dreamed we'd be this far apart.* Each time he pondered such thoughts, Alan's anger was pricked; *I've got to fight off these negatives. They can't be happening,* he would tell himself.

Alan's anger can be understood as directly linked to the ideals he held for the relationship with his son. His desires were normal, even commendable; but they were the basis for wishful thinking, which set him up to feel disillusioned. The angrier he grew toward his son, the more it indicated an unwillingness to let go of those wishful desires. As Alan continued his consultations with Dr. Minirth, several of these driving wishes came to light:

- Conversations with Jeron typified by mutual respect
- Mature listening skills, where Jeron would show that he was fully integrating his dad's perspectives
- Fun times when he and his son would laugh and enjoy good humor
- Obedient and appreciative response in matters of discipline
- Strong similarities in personal values and priorities

Can you relate to Alan's wishful thinking? Through the years, what ideals have you held most dear regarding your relationship with your children? (For instance, "I had always hoped that our family could have fair-minded discussions when it was obvious we didn't fully agree about something," or "I wanted to have the deep sharing with my daughter that I was never able to have with my parents.")

_____

_____

_____

Can you recognize that your anger is provoked when you are led into conflict with your children because the relationship has fallen short of those ideals? How is your anger connected to disappointment because ideals have not been satisfied? (For instance, "I never thought I'd have to respond to a smart-mouthed child, and when my daughter is sassy it flies all over me," or "I become frustrated with my son when I see him put such a low priority on a good education; that's not what I want for him.")

_____

_____

_____

It is both good and necessary to have lofty goals for your children. It can also be dangerous. Angry parents have often turn their ideals into a pattern called _mythical thinking,_ which is defined as the tendency to overlook reality because of a craving to create ideal circumstances.

To get an idea of your capability for mythical thinking, look over this list of ingredients commonly found in this pattern. Place a check next to the statements that apply fairly frequently.

_____ Statements such as "I can't believe . . ." or "Why can't you just . . ."

_____ Loaded questions such as "What is wrong with you?" or "Why do you keep doing that?"

_____ Pleading with the child to be more reasonable

_____ Comparative statements such as "When I was your age I never . . ."

_____ Disillusionment caused by your child's lack of cooperation

———— Readiness to concede defeat: "I just give up"

———— Repeated referral to the way things ought to be

———— Inability to accept your child's dissenting thoughts

———— Labeling the child's differing preferences as wrong or bad

———— Demanding loyalty as a payback: "After all the nice things I've done for you . . ."

When mythical thinking is in gear, parents can have such strong ideals that it becomes difficult to make room for many of the competing attitudes or differing choices that commonly accompany a child's reaction to the parent. If you relate to at least five of the ingredients listed here, your anger is probably unnecessarily intensified, thanks to your insistence that the relationship should be devoid of the real issues so typical between parent and child.

What behaviors do you exhibit that show you are holding to myths as you relate to your children? (For instance, "I'm too easily dismayed when my son displays a noncooperative spirit," or "I plead with my daughter to please act respectfully toward me.")

_____

_____

_____

Trading Myths for Truth

An extensive encounter between Jesus and the Pharisees is recorded in John 8. Jesus was explaining to them his identity and mission, but they did not grasp his words at all. They asked various questions, and each time he answered they illustrated how their biases were so strong that they were unable to accept what he was telling them. At the end of the exchange, Jesus turned to his followers and said, "You shall know the truth and the truth shall set you free" (John 8:32). He was underscoring the necessity of approaching life with enough objectivity that we can weigh out the facts carefully to determine how to proceed.

Each time you recognize that a myth is lurking beneath your agitation toward one of your children, be willing to ponder the truth that you are trying to deny. It could be that you have such a strong preference for a specific response that you are unwilling to objectively discern the best path to take. Sometimes you may be required to incorporate *ugly truth*, meaning you must accept facts that are not what you want. For instance, Jeron would indicate that he'd rather spend time with his friends, even if it meant ignoring family interests, and Alan would easily become angry. "I just can't understand why he finds it so easy to disregard the need for family time," he would grumble. He was ignoring the truth that teenagers can have such a hunger for peer acceptance that it can cause them to seem rude or disinterested when faced with the prospect of giving up social activities for family interactions. Alan was not wrong for wanting quality time with his son, but his anger would be less severe if he dropped his myths and incorporated truth, even if it were truth he did not like.

Let's examine some of the myths that predictably fuel anger in the home.

> *Myth:* Kids should learn to obey after the first time they are told.
> *Truth:* Much repetition is required before children grasp lessons.

Recall when your children were just learning to write the alphabet. You would make a large *A*, and then you would hand the pencil to the child and say, "Now, you make one just like I did." How skilled was the child in performing good penmanship? Usually it takes years of daily practice before a child's penmanship is smooth and adultlike. (Many grownup children *still* display poor habits in this effort.) Reasonable expectations are required as you recognize that a child will not do perfectly while honing simple skills.

How much more complex it is for a child to learn the intricacies of relationships and management of emotions. Beginning in the early years, parents can give instructions regarding the wisest way to maneuver through complicated relationships, yet one or two discussions are never enough to guarantee that the child will figure it all out. As in learning penmanship, hundreds of practice efforts are needed before the skills become second nature. This means great patience is necessary on the part of the parents.

Each time Jeron spoke combatively to his dad, Alan would think, *What's the deal with this kid? How many times do I have to tell him that his abrasiveness won't fly?* Alan seemed truly baffled that his sixteen-year-old would not receive his words of instruction and make the necessary adjustment.

Dr. Minirth spoke with Alan about his annoyance: "I certainly don't want to indicate that you should never feel frustrated when your son speaks venomously to you. That truly is a hurtful experience. What I *do* want to emphasize is patience. Each time you respond gruffly toward him, the learning process is lengthened. You may have to remind him many more times before he buys into the validity of your thoughts. In the meantime, you'll be required to maintain a steady disposition as you give him room to learn."

In what circumstances do you talk to yourself about the hope that your children will learn better behavior more quickly? (For instance, "I've told my daughter a hundred times not to be so bossy, but it's like she's never heard me say it," or "It's been years since I first told my son that he should treat his sister better, and he still doesn't get it.")

_____

_____

_____

How is your anger affected for the better if you hold firmly to your assertions but with more patient awareness that it will take time before you see the full results? (For instance, "I wouldn't be so pushy even as I speak my convictions," or "I'd be willing to discuss the better options as each anger-provoking circumstance arises.")

_____

_____

_____

To develop patience toward your children's immature use of anger, you need look no further than to your own inconsistencies in anger management as you realize that it is not an easy thing to perfect relationship skills. Parents often lose credibility by insisting that their children act correctly even as they (the parents) continue to display poor skills in expressing themselves. Parents gain credibility, however, by talking with their kids from a personal frame of reference regarding the difficulties associated with learning emotional management.

For instance, Alan made a breakthrough with Jeron when he spoke candidly with his son about his own inconsistencies: "I know I sound impatient sometimes when I ask you to be more respectful of my requirements for our home. Being honest, though, I've got to admit that I'm not always perfect either as I deal with conflict, so I should cut you some slack, even as I would hope you'd do the same for me. Based on my own track record, I realize it will take time for you to be the way I'd like you to be. I'm willing to hang in there and work it through with you. Are you willing to work with me on getting it right?"

Are you ever willing to display the same patience? How might this affect the atmosphere in your home? (For instance, "We'd probably be less insulting or condescending as we speak with each other," or "Hopefully, my daughter would be a little less defensive.")

_____

_____

_____

Myth: Gentleness implies weakness.
Truth: Gentleness can be strength on full display.

As we talk with parents who want to diminish their children's tendency toward strong anger, we emphasize calm confidence. It is ironic that in speaking with their children about desisting from abrasive anger, they display the very abrasiveness they disdain in their children. Rather than listening only to the words spoken by the parents, the children listen to the emotional pitch that accompanies the words. Any inconsistency on the parents' part ensures that their children will not heed what is said.

In discussing the mannerisms of those who yield to the direction of the Spirit, the apostle Paul specifically warned against such traits as contentiousness, angry outbursts, and dissension. He then went on to say that the fruit of the Spirit is displayed in the softer traits of love, joy, peace, patience, kindness, gentleness, faithfulness, goodness, and self-control (see Galatians 5:19–23). These qualities are certainly not what parents feel during tension with their young, but a commitment to be God's servant can result in the willingness to let go of natural tension in favor of his direction.

Given the tension that usually accompanies moments of angry conflict, it can be most unnatural for parents to respond calmly. Nevertheless, that is precisely what is needed. Consider the analogy of a paramedic arriving upon an accident scene. The victims are moaning in pain and in desperate need of someone to assist them in the effort to heal. Suddenly the paramedic begins shouting in a panic, "How could this happen? What in the world did you do to get yourself into such a fine mess? How can you expect me to help you if you keep moaning in pain?" A trained paramedic understands the necessity of a calm spirit. Even as she observes great disaster, her demeanor is not excitable, but steady.

The same strength is required when parents engage with their children in a potential emotional disaster. Even if the child is explosive or insulting, the parent does not need to respond in kind. Gentle firmness is the most powerful component in such an incident.

Alan admitted that the adjustment from harshness to gentleness was a difficult challenge as he attempted to change his responses to Jeron's undesirable behavior. Dr. Minirth spoke words of encouragement: "Whether he admits it or not, Jeron wants to see that you know what you're doing when you respond in moments of conflict. If you act as erratically as he does, it instills no confidence at all in him. When you deliver a message about responsibility or respectfulness in an even tone of voice, you communicate that you believe in yourself and your message. That's a display of strength that he needs."

Have you ever thought of calm confidence as being a display of weakness? What falsehoods have you latched onto that cause you to think that way? (For instance, "I've been trained to think that the one who can overpower the other in a conflict is the winner," or "It seems that my daughter only responds to me when my voice is at peak volume.")

_____

_____

_____

Through the years, how have your children responded as you try to display strength by way of the overpowering approach? (For instance, "In her earlier years my daughter complied, but now she's openly oppositional," or "My son is not shy about going toe-to-toe with me.")

_____

_____

_____

How can your approach to anger management improve if you take an approach that relies more on gentle firmness? (For instance, "I could still stand my ground without getting caught in nonproductive, circular arguments," or "My discussions with my son would be less defensive as I hold firmly but without persuasion to my convictions.")

_____

_____

_____

As calmness and gentleness become part of your demeanor, you show your child that you are sufficiently secure in your beliefs that you can refrain from begging or pleading with the child to take you seriously. Realize that your kids will not necessarily drop their immature behaviors immediately, and then proceed with the confidence that in the absence of coercive communication they have a greater opportunity to ponder the validity of the message you are attempting to convey.

> *Myth:* When my children are angry with me, it means they are rejecting me.
> *Truth:* The anger of children is most often a sign of hurt or confusion.

One reason parents respond poorly to their children's anger is the assumption that the youngster's anger signifies rejection of the parent. The child's harsh responses can strike the parents at their place of insecurity, with the result that the parent ceases to focus on the problem at hand while he or she unnecessarily defends personal dignity.

Alan learned that his correct anger was sometimes derailed as he responded too sensitively to Jeron's lack of cooperation. If he gave Jeron a directive, his son would often reply with a complaint. Immediately Alan might retort, "Why do you have to be so belligerent when I ask you to do something?" In responding this way, the original request is put on hold as Alan shifts the attention onto the rejecting element of Jeron's response.

Through counseling, Alan learned that he did not have to wince as if his self-esteem were at issue every time Jeron spoke words of disagreement. For instance, there were numerous past incidents when Jeron would use such words as *ridiculous, stupid,* or *idiotic* in reacting to instructions given to him by one of his parents. With his anger on a very short fuse, Alan would react strongly and negatively to those words; in effect his response communicated, "How dare you refer to me as ridiculous."

As part of his effort to decrease his anger intensity, Alan learned not to personalize Jeron's insulting or rejecting words. Clinging to the realization that he was not ridiculous, stupid, or idiotic, Alan learned to bypass the insult and focus instead on the reason Jeron felt angry. He developed a deeper appreciation that God was on his side; armed with such a positive thought he did not need to panic if Jeron indicated he had low regard for him in the moment. He could say: "Jeron, I know it seems stupid to you that I would require you to make better grades before you can have full weekend privileges. That's one of my values that you don't yet appreciate fully. I also know how important it is for you to feel connected to your friends. I'm willing to work with you so you can regain your privileges; nonetheless, I'm still going to hold you to my academic expectations. I know this is something we can work on together." Alan found that he did not have to yell or act as if his son were threatening his authority. Focusing on his son's hurt as opposed to his own feelings of rejection, his conflict management style was more open to good communication.

When do you tend to interpret your child's lack of cooperation as rejection? (For instance, "My daughter insists on dating a young man I don't like, and I take it to mean that she rejects me and my values," or "My son mocks my spiritual values, and it feels as if he is ashamed of who I am.")

_____

_____

_____

Consider that your child's disagreement could stem from issues beyond rejecting you. What other factors may lie beneath your child's defiance? (For instance, "My daughter chooses guys who are not good for her because she struggles to feel secure," or "My son mocks my religion because he's confused about anything related to God.")

_____

_____

_____

If you choose to set aside your feelings of rejection and focus instead on the other issues beneath your child's contrary reactions, how will your anger management be improved? (For instance, "My communication would be less defensive and more understanding," or "I would illustrate to my kids that I want to know where they hurt emotionally.")

_____

_____

_____

Even when your children seem most disagreeable or defiant, there is still a strong probability that they want you to remain in the parental role. Their anger can be understood as a cry of confusion or hurt. Inevitably, they are struggling to determine where their real values lie. You are more influential in choosing not to make your acceptability the issue and showing instead a willingness to discuss the child's hurts and needs.

> _Myth:_ Good families don't have anger problems.
> _Truth:_ No family is ever completely synchronized to the point of having zero conflict.

When parents respond poorly to their children's contrariness, there is usually a form of pessimism in play. "Oh no," the reasoning goes. "This can't be happening. My child and our family life are falling apart right in front of my eyes." Spurred by such thinking, parents push hard to force their child not to be disagreeable. The net result is increased emotional combustion.

Recall Sandra, whose fourteen-year-old daughter, Bethany, was highly extroverted and plugged in with her friends but openly rude to her mother's requests for a coordinated family life. When Bethany challenged her mother's decisions (which was frequent), Sandra seemed to operate with disbelief that her daughter could be so haughty. She told Dr. Carter, "That is *definitely* not the way I have taught her to believe."

The doctor replied, "I get the distinct feeling that you believe you have missed the mark as a parent each time Bethany is argumentative." She nodded in clear agreement. He continued: "Let's recognize that Bethany's foul moods do not indicate that you're a failure, or that she's a lost cause. She's fourteen years old, and it's very common for people of that age to act as if they've finally got life figured out. She wants to have more and more autonomy, which means that she assumes she needs your input less and less. Rather than assuming that your family is now headed for disaster, let's take into account the reality that she's feeling her own way toward maturity. Predictably, she'll make misjudgments along the way, but that's not a formula for disaster. When the two of you are at odds, you can use it as a time to discuss her beliefs in a sane manner. Even if she's misguided, you can still maintain optimism from the realization that she's on a learning curve. Her philosophy of life is not set in cement yet."

Beginning in the preteens and continuing throughout adolescence, young people grow more aware that their parents do not hold all the wisdom of the world. Their growing awareness of different values joins their increased ability to think outside the box, and it sometimes causes the young person to disagree with the priorities and values of the parents. Rather than shutting the young person down at such a time, are you willing to use a moment of disagreement to calmly discuss your child's reasoning?

For instance, Sandra realized it did no good to assume the worst when Bethany displayed differing preferences. Her "otherness" did not mean that she was a bad daughter, or that their family cohesion had dis-integrated. One Saturday when Sandra learned that Bethany had gone out the prior night with girls she did not want her to be with, she chose not to berate her daughter. Instead, she spoke calmly: "Bethany, despite knowing that I didn't want you to go to Cassie's house last night, you chose to go anyway. That tells me that it must be a real big deal for you to go out with her. Help me understand the appeal."

When Bethany became predictably defensive, Sandra gently put her hand up and said, "I'm not looking for a fight. I'm truly trying to un-derstand your way of thinking. Talk with me about your needs, because I want to know how you and I can become more coordinated." This ap-proach was quite novel, and Bethany noticed that her mother's tone of voice was genuinely nonthreatening. A dialogue opened between the two that was much more constructive than their normal bickering.

How can you tell if you are nursing the myth that your family should have no conflict or anger problems? (For instance, "I'll admit that I'm too quickly agitated when my daughter is contrary, as if she should al-ways have the same values as me," or "I rarely slow down to discern why my son feels angry; I just act overwhelming.")

_____

_____

_____

How do your anger responses differ if you accept that your child can become angry, and sometimes irrationally so? (For instance, "I'd focus less on my son's anger outbursts and concentrate more on why he feels hurt," or "I'd talk more freely with my children about the normalcy of differing preferences.")

_____

_____

_____

When you accept the reality of anger at home, the intensity of it actu-ally diminishes.

Myth: When tempers flair, it means the rest of the day is ruined.

Truth: You can get back on track even after a family member displays a disagreeable emotion.

All-or-nothing thinking is quite common in families that frequently mishandle anger. Rather than recognizing how emotions can be experienced in many forms and with varying degrees of intensity, they tend to use tunnel vision as they respond to one another. For instance, whenever Sandra encountered Bethany's abrupt anger, she would react as if Bethany were little more than a chronically agitated person. She would forget that Bethany could also be friendly, forgiving, and confident. Her snappy responses reflected an overly negative assessment of her daughter. Once she communicated her irritation toward Bethany, she was slow to return to a normal mode of relating. Her pessimism would influence her responses for hours to come.

What evidence indicates that you have allowed yourself to respond to anger with lingering pessimism? (For instance, "I have very little patience when my son makes misjudgments, even when they are minor," or "If my daughter and I disagree, we may remain stuck in a cycle of annoyance for the next several hours.")

_____

_____

_____

When anger is experienced with your children, the emotion does not have to become a defining aspect of the relationship. Though the anger indicates that you are at odds with one another, it does not mean that the entire relationship is adversarial. It means you bring differences to the relationship, and that is not fatal.

Sandra was able to display good awareness in a discussion with Dr. Carter as she reflected on an angry exchange she had recently had with Bethany. "After we finished our disagreement," she said, "we went our separate ways for a while, and I must admit that I was doing some major pouting. A couple of hours later, Bethany asked me about an entirely different matter, and her tone of voice was normal. I wasn't finished with my sulking and I almost replied to her with some left-over irritation. But that's when it hit me. I can remain stuck in my bad mood and when Bethany is ready to be normal with me again, I am tempted to pull her back into the anger mode. I've got to be careful because if I do that too often she's likely to be perpetually angry with me, and that's certainly not what our family needs."

Sandra was on target with her awareness. It is a reality that parents and kids disagree, and sometimes they do so in an unpleasant way. It is also a reality that those same parents and kids can respect each other and be cooperative. One reality does not cancel the other. Families are a mixed bag of both good and bad ingredients. This means they should not be so enamored with the good times that they try to cling desperately to them, nor should they live in such dread of the negative times that they assume they are doomed to be forever miserable with each other.

If you firmly accept the reality that your relationship with your kids will have mixed results, how can that diminish anger's hold on you? (For instance, "When my son acts as if he despises me, I can find peace by remembering that there are things I do that he really appreciates," or "If my daughter and I can't agree on her dress habits, I can recall that we have had other conversations that illustrate respect for each other's opinions.")

_____

_____

_____

As you work to keep the mood of anger from lingering too long, what do you hope you can teach your children? (For instance, "I want to make sure my daughter understands that I don't just love her in the good times, I love her even when things are rocky," or "It's important that my son knows that even in a disagreement we can still resolve to show respect to one another.")

_____

_____

_____

Myth: Rebellious young people become dysfunctional adults.

Truth: When rebellion occurs, it can set the stage for the maturity process to deepen.

A goal of parenting is to prepare young people to become successful adults. Parents work hard to instill values and responsibility into their kids because they recognize that childhood is the time when the foundation is laid for all sorts of important habits and attitudes. Each act of discipline is a lesson that can bring dividends years later.

Knowing this, parents may cringe when they feel that their foundation-laying efforts are going to waste. When parents learn that their children are picking up irresponsible behaviors, or are experimenting with poor ethics and morality, or are failing to see the necessity of solid work habits, they may be inclined to press harder than ever to make the children conform. The result can be increased anger for both the parent and the child.

It is good when parents maintain consistent teachings regarding values and responsibility, but that teaching need not be accompanied by fear that the young person will become an abject failure. Alan spoke with Dr. Minirth about his reasons for riding Jeron about his work habits. "Right now," he explained, "Jeron's greatest concerns should be his assignments for school and the responsibilities associated with his part-time job. I swear, I can get pretty agitated at that boy because every time he slacks off, I'm thinking about how tough life is going to be for him when he's an adult who still has lousy work habits."

"I certainly can't argue with your logic," came the reply, "since I too believe in the necessity of teaching your son to take his responsibilities seriously."

Alan admitted, "I'm starting to realize that when he and I get caught in one of our nonproductive dances of anger, it's propelled by my concerns about his future."

"Maybe you've got too much of a good thing," the doctor reflected. "If your aspirations for your son's future keep you in unhealthy patterns of anger, perhaps you should do yourself and Jeron a favor and worry a little less about what lies ahead."

How do your concerns about your child's future cause you to become overzealous in your anger? (For instance, "When I think about my daughter being seduced by immoral attitudes, I worry that she'll become an adult with lots of regrets," or "I want my son to be able to support himself once he finishes school, but every time I witness his laziness I know he's digging himself into a deep hole.")

_____

_____

_____

It is not wrong to be concerned about your child's future, but that concern does not need to be displayed in anger. Looking back into your own past, you can probably recognize that much of your own personal maturation occurred as a direct result of poor choices you made. It is never a delight to witness your own children in rebellion against good values; however, you need not pressure them to learn the fullness of truth right away. You can still apply consequences when necessary, and you can certainly make time for advice-giving discussions. These efforts are most effective, though, when your anger is minimized and your fear about their future is balanced by an appreciation for lessons learned in the aftermath of failure.

How will your anger diminish if you make room for the possibility of rebellion even as you continue to speak about good values and apply reasonable consequences? (For instance, "I'd lecture less, and I'd remember that time needs to pass before some people can appreciate truth," or "I'd be careful not to let pessimism creep into my attitude toward my son, even when I'm disappointed.")

_____

_____

_____

A primary truth that dispels all of the myths of parenting is that no family is perfect. Anytime your children display imperfection and when you do too, take consolation in knowing that learning can be the result.

For Family Discussion

1. Have each family member identify three or four ideals that are not likely to come true within your family unit.

2. Let each person describe how he or she tends to handle frustration each time the person comes to realize that those ideals are not going to be met.

3. If you learn to incorporate "ugly truth," you can be more patient. Go around the room, focusing one at a time on each family member and identify at least three ways that person can act more patiently.

4. Anger does not always mean that you are rejecting the other person; it may be that you feel hurt or confused. What hurts cause you to feel angry, and how would you like the other family members to show they understand your hurt?

5. It's true that even good families experience anger. Sometimes, however, the anger can cause us to forget what is good. Focus one at a time on each family member and name at least five things that are good about the person.

For Further Reflection

In describing how heathens continue in sin, Paul recorded (in Romans 1:25): "They exchanged the truth of God for a lie."

1. What are some myths (lies) that we wish for as we try to maintain an ideal family life? Why do we allow ourselves to be sidetracked by those myths?

2. When we allow myths to inhibit us from accepting unwanted realities, how does this help create anger? In your anger, what truths are you force-feeding your children that they are not willing to receive?

Jeremiah 17:9 reminds us: "The heart is more deceitful than all else and is desperately sick; who can understand it?"

3. What unflattering truths about your children do you have difficulty accepting? What are some unflattering truths about yourself that your kids have difficulty accepting?

4. How will the emotional climate in your home change for the better if you consistently talk with your kids about the flaws in each family member that need improvement? What is the difference between accusing your kids and having constructive discussion about the effects of sin?

John 1:14 describes Christ as being "full of grace and truth."

5. How do you know that you are discussing necessary truths with your kids while also maintaining an attitude of grace? How does a spirit of grace affect your management of anger?

6. If you drop your myths, you are more likely to be open to insight into the real motives that drive your children's anger. What can you learn about your kids if you seek more consistently to understand the meaning behind their anger? How will the tendency toward defensiveness diminish if your family grows more capable of speaking truth?

11

DISPLACED ANGER

STEP 11: *Identify your own outside stressors that create anger, and choose to address them separately, as opposed to bringing them into parental communication.*

L et's suppose that someone becomes angry with you and strongly speaks rejecting words. As the frustration flows, you get the distinct impression that the person is actually angry about something entirely different, yet he is channeling all his emotions toward you. Has this ever happened? If so, you have experienced displacement, the shifting of emotional tension toward someone who is not directly involved in creating the tension.

Judy was an expressive woman in her mid-forties who sought counseling from Dr. Carter because of anxiety attacks that often left her feeling emotionally and physically drained. Looking like someone who felt she was carrying the weight of the world on her shoulders, she was animated as she spoke about her difficulty in making it from one day to the next. She had an eleven-year-old daughter, Amanda, and a fourteen-year-old son, Josh. In addition to all of the responsibilities involved in getting them from one activity to the next, she owned an interior design business. It was a part-time job and had very flexible hours, but there were many moments when she needed to be in two places at the same time.

"I'm moody and uptight most of the time," she explained to the doctor. "I love my kids and I love my work, but too often it's more than I can bear when I try to wear two hats at once. Yesterday was a perfect example of the way my days can be. Josh had a basketball game at six o'clock, so I wanted him to get a start on his homework before he had to leave the house. He's normally a good student, but he's just not catching on to algebra, which means I really have to work with him so he won't lose heart. Amanda had dance lessons at four o'clock, and it takes twenty minutes one way to get her there, so that ate up time I needed to be spending with Josh. In the meantime, I had a customer breathing down my neck because we were putting in new curtains in her dining room and living room. She wasn't pleased with the way it was looking, so I was on the cell phone listening to her complaints, and then I had to call my supplier to see if she could help me calm that lady down. In the meantime, we were so pushed for time that we didn't get supper until after eight o'clock, after Josh's game. My days aren't always that tight, but it's not really uncommon either."

"Where was your husband during this whirlwind of activity?"

"Well, yesterday he was out of town. He's gone overnight maybe three or four nights per month. But even when he's in town he's not much help. He stays super busy at his job, and most evenings he doesn't get home until seven o'clock or so. He tries to make it to some of the kids' activities, but his world is so unpredictable that I can't really count on him."

"Tell me the effect of all this on your mood."

"Well, that's why I'm here. I get really tense almost every day. My kids complain because I'm too wired. Josh has told me point blank that he doesn't want me to help him with homework because I just make him nervous. I'm edgy and get irritated way too easily, and I'm afraid I appear impatient most of the time. Every morning at our house, there is a distinct possibility that *someone* is going to explode. Either I'll bark at one of the kids or my husband will yell at me or one of them. Josh and Amanda frequently go to school with scowls on their faces because they've been fussed at for something minor. Our house is chaos and something has to be done to ease the frustration!"

Do Judy's circumstances have a ring of familiarity? What lifestyle demands regularly churn up irritability or frustration in your home? (For instance, "My children are constantly on the go and I have to be creative at times to keep up with their needs," or "My husband and I see things differently when it comes to disciplining the children, and this keeps us in a constant state of frustration.")

_____

_____

_____

How do these strains affect your management of anger? (For instance, "I stay snippy when I'm with my daughter because I can never get her cooperation," or "I try to keep up the appearance of calm, but deep down inside I resent being pulled by so many outside influences.")

_____

_____

_____

When outside pressures create stress, the most common emotional response is anger. True to the definition of anger, the need to preserve personal worth, needs, and convictions is great. A common problem with this stress is that the angry person does not do what is necessary to confront the stress-producing situation but instead allows the emotions to spill onto relatively innocent recipients.

Dr. Carter explained to Judy: "I'm sure you're aware of the stereotype of the person who is angry at the boss at work, but instead of speaking to the boss he goes home and kicks the dog. That's the picture that comes to mind when I hear you describing your anxiety. For instance, you may be annoyed because of a difficult customer, but your daughter or son is the one who catches the brunt of your anger. Or perhaps you're frustrated because you are not getting your husband's reinforcement, but if you don't successfully resolve your tensions with him, the kids can receive the spill-over."

"That describes me to a T," Judy replied. "I've got so many things churning in my mind that I'm scattered as I try to deal with all my issues."

Going to Anger's Real Source

Exodus 18 records an interesting story about how Moses' father-in-law, Jethro, had to help his son-in-law rearrange his priorities so he could be a more effective leader. By this time in his life, Moses had become the ultimate parental figure for the people of Israel, and when disputes arose they lined up to get his opinion. The people were so insistent on having his attention that they would wait all day long if necessary to speak with him. When Jethro came to pay a family visit, he saw that Moses was so taxed by the people's demands that he was unable to even say hello. In essence, Jethro was told he had to take a number and wait his turn to talk with Moses.

Once he finally gained an audience with his son-in-law, Jethro stated simply but firmly, "This thing you do is not good." He then helped Moses devise a system of judges, whereby Moses could be relieved of many of the nitpicky demands that drained him so he could focus instead on the things that mattered most. Jethro wisely recognized that individuals who stretch themselves too far are in danger of becoming ineffective in their responsibilities.

When we work with people like Judy, a primary goal is to identify the external causes of the anger to address them directly. We often learn that they are so stretched in the rigors of life that an inner build-up of tension is inevitable. If changes are not made for the purpose of simplifying daily demands, anger will predictably be displaced onto undeserving victims. Are you willing to adjust your lifestyle for the purpose of diminishing the potential for displaced anger? Let's look at several areas that may need examination.

Overloaded Schedules

Compare the schedule demands on today's young people with those of people who were youths in the 1950s, 1960s, and 1970s. Those past generations certainly were not void of outside stimulation, but today's children by comparison are on the fast track. Beginning as early as age three or four, children are placed into sports and other organized events by parents who do not want to deprive them of opportunities to get ahead. This is the beginning of a youngster's lifestyle defined by schedules. All the way through the grade school, junior high, and high school years, one organized group after another vies for the attention of children and their parents. If parents indicate that they do not deem all their children's events as necessary, great pressure comes upon them from the kids, their friends, or other parents. "You can't deprive our youth of wholesome activities," the reasoning goes. "To limit your children's organized activities is tantamount to neglect!"

Has your family ever been stressed from schedules that have gotten out of control? What are some examples? (For instance, "My son plays sports year round, plus he is involved in a demanding choir program at school, as well as all the youth activities at church," or "My daughter is invited to countless birthday parties, she has heavy homework because of her advanced placement classes, and she's on the volleyball team and the school drill team. I barely spend any quality time with her.")

_____

_____

_____

_____

Judy told Dr. Carter: "I want my kids to have good memories of their childhood, so it's important to me that they are involved in the right activities." Heaving a deep sigh she added, "It's all I can do, though, to keep up with them. The older they get, the more opportunities they have to stay busy. That just means more driving for me, and I'm also on them constantly because they seem to forget that schoolwork has to take priority over all their extracurricular activities. I'll bet I get into a major argument at least once a day with each of them over the juggling of demands, and it might happen several times per day."

When you are on schedule overload, how does it affect your anger? (For instance, "I've been very impatient lately with my daughter because she lags behind as I try to push her to get everything done that has to be done," or "My son doesn't have good organizational skills, so I'm constantly arguing with him about what needs to be done next.")

_____

_____

_____

Amid this busyness, how are your children's moods affected? (For instance, "My daughter can be *very* hateful when she feels I'm pushing her to do what she doesn't want to do," or "My son is openly aggressive, and he might throw things if he feels crowded.")

_____

_____

_____

Dr. Carter told Judy, "I'm sure it seems insane sometimes when you're so pressured with the kids' activities that you have little time for rewarding family time." At that Judy scoffed and said, "Rewarding family time! What's that?"

The doctor made his point. "I'm afraid you're not unlike many other American families who are so driven by overloaded schedules that the relationships suffer greatly. I can teach you all sorts of concepts about the inner workings of anger, but until you pare down the schedule, none of those concepts will help."

It is both good and necessary to teach your children that they cannot have it all or do it all. Judy decided it was time for a serious talk with Josh and Amanda about how their moods had become so tense because of their schedule overload. "Beginning next semester, I'm going to have to limit each of you to one major outside involvement," she told them. "Each of you has three or four interests pulling on you, but you'll have to decide which one means the most." Both kids complained about her decision, but instead of arguing about the merits of her reasoning Judy calmly held her ground. "That's the decision I've made and I'm sticking to it. In a couple of days I'll ask you what your final choice will be."

Later, she told the doctor, "It was interesting. Both Josh and Amanda complained when I talked about establishing schedule limits, but I don't think either was shocked at my decision. It's like they knew we had to make the adjustment, and they had been quietly wondering when I would say what I said."

Your children may not be as compliant as Judy's, but are you willing to be the one to restore sanity to your schedule? How might you accomplish it? (For instance, "I need to talk with my kids about choosing the single most important activity and let that be enough," or "We need to determine that there will be breaks in between various sports seasons, no year-round team events.")

_____

_____

_____

When you meet resistance from your kids, keep in mind that the more you debate the more you empower their anger. Stand firmly in the realization that your assertion makes sense, and, like Judy, refrain from defending your position if you see it only feeds an argumentative atmosphere. Draw strength from the realization that young people can benefit greatly by learning to give more quality attention to fewer requirements.

Poor Time Management

It was a typical school morning at Judy's home, which meant that she was prodding both Amanda and Josh to get in the car on time. Eleven-year-old Amanda was close to tears because she could not find the shoes she wanted to wear. Finally, they were spotted under a chair in the family room, so as she struggled to tie the laces her mom was saying, "Hurry up, we're already a couple of minutes behind."

As Amanda picked up her backpack, her mom casually asked, "You _did_ brush your teeth, didn't you?" Amanda had not. She'd overslept that morning and barely had time to wolf down a bowl of cereal. She was not known for being speedy anyway as she showered and put on the day's clothes. Judy followed her back into the bathroom to make sure she did not dally in brushing her teeth. When she entered Amanda's room, her frustration increased as she discovered a wet towel on the floor alongside Amanda's pajamas and various other articles of clothing. When she complained to her daughter, Amanda whined sourly, "I'm doing the best I can, but I just don't have time to be as perfect as you want me to be." As you might imagine, the rest of the rush time was defined by griping and fuming. Sound familiar?

Many families have good intentions regarding time management and the organization that goes along with it, but it does not always culminate in successful implementation. For instance, Judy wanted Amanda to be in bed each night by 9:30 so she could get close to the nine hours of sleep she needed. Being older, Josh was to be in bed between 10:00 and 10:30. They were also to give priority to homework over other interests (gabbing on the phone, playing on the computer). These things rarely happened as planned, but that is how Judy wanted it to be. Instead, the kids were lax in getting ready for bed, meaning they were often late. Mornings were usually hectic because they did not get up with the alarm clock. Too often, school projects were put aside, which meant Judy would argue with them about their irresponsibility.

When do you find that time is poorly managed in your household? (For instance, "My daughter is notorious for waiting until the last minute to tackle a major homework assignment," or "My son wastes time in computer chat rooms, and it compromises his ability to manage the rest of his responsibilities.")

_____

_____

_____

When you and your children are in a time crunch, what effect does this have on the anger in the home? (For instance, "My kids and I are frequently tense because someone has been wasting time and causing problems for everyone else," or "Mornings are awful because I can't persuade my son to get up when he's supposed to.")

Dr. Carter explained to Judy: "When you consistently express exasperation toward Amanda regarding her tardiness in the morning, she learns that you are the one, not she, who is most emotionally invested in her choices. That needs to be reversed so she'll learn to take the lead in her own well-being."

"But how do I do that? I've talked with her on countless occasions about being more reliable in her time management, but within two or three days it's as if the discussion never occurred. I just can't get through to her."

"Well, first," replied the doctor, "you'll need to get used to the reality that you have to watch the clock for her and be a prompter of sorts, even as you expect her to make an improved effort. You'll need to be consistent in remembering the discipline she predictably forgets. For instance, early in the evening you'll have to check with her about her school assignments and as she's doing her work stay in touch with her progress. At around eight-thirty, prompt her to begin preparing for bed, changing clothes, picking up her room, and all that goes along with bedtime. That way, she'll have a better chance to stay on schedule. She needs your direction."

"But she's so poky," Judy said; "I can't always get her to comply. Besides, when I do what you're suggesting, I feel like the ultimate nag. What am I supposed to do to keep from coming off like a drill sergeant?"

"That's where consequences come in," said Dr. Carter. "Let her know that if at the end of the day she hasn't succeeded in following the guidelines, the next day will bring a loss of television privileges. Also, you can establish rewards, like letting her pick out a favorite place to have a weekend meal if she's complied with the schedule throughout the week."

Yelling, pleading, and threatening are options as you attempt to teach time management to your kids. Be prepared, though, to discover that these options are usually accompanied by a great amount of wasted anger. A calm statement of consequences followed by effective follow-through is also an option. When you persuade, you are in the position of taking on the burden of making your child comply. If you calmly, yet firmly, apply consequences, the burden of compliance is shifted to the child. The key, of course, is consistency, consistency, consistency.

What consequences can you implement to reinforce the necessity of good time management? (For instance, "If my son is up late working on a term paper he procrastinated on, I'm going to bed at my usual time and he'll have computer privileges suspended for a couple of days," or "If my daughter is late for cheerleader practice, I'll let her experience the consequences given by the school, and we'll choose an activity to remove from her calendar so it won't be so crowded.")

_____

_____

_____

Your kids probably won't like it when you let consequences run their course. What good options do you have at such a time so you will not get caught in an angry battle? (For instance, "Rather than pleading my case, I can calmly state that I'm satisfied with my decision," or "I can involve my kids in advance in the decision regarding the possible consequences that will accompany their poor use of time.")

_____

_____

_____

Strained Outside Relationships

Anger is often expressed toward a family member when in fact it has been generated in an outside relationship. True to the nature of displacement, the angry person usually feels less safe handling the emotion in its proper context, so it is unloaded on a family member.

Being fourteen, Josh was interested in a girl at school, but he felt ill-equipped to know how to handle the young lady's mixed signals. One day, Courtney would act interested and flirtatious toward Josh, and the next she would ignore him altogether. One afternoon, as Judy was

trying to map out the rest of the day's plans, Josh was particularly edgy
and uncooperative. She tried to talk with him about the need for coordination. Josh snapped at her, "Look, I don't need you telling me what
to do! I'll take care of my own responsibilities. Just leave me alone!"

Later, while watching one of Josh's basketball games, Judy learned
from another mother that Courtney had turned Josh down when he invited her to meet him at the coming Friday evening gathering. Her
immediate thought was, *No wonder Josh was so grouchy this afternoon. He was
embarrassed by being turned down by Courtney.* Later, when she talked with
Josh about it, he confirmed what had happened, and they were able to
have a good discussion.

When have you had an angry exchange in your home that was the
byproduct of frustration your children had with people away from home?
(For instance, "My daughter feels she isn't accepted by her peers at school,
and this leaves her feeling discouraged and moody," or "The boys my
son hangs out with are very boisterous, and they feed a rebellious streak
in him, to the extent that he seems mad at the world.")

_____

_____

_____

You cannot solve the issues that exist between your kids and their friends,
but you can certainly choose not to become ensnared by their erratic
emotions. For instance, when Josh spoke rudely to Judy prior to going
to the basketball game, she could have put her own hurt feelings out
in the open. She might have complained, "Why do you feel you can talk
to me like this? I'm not putting up with your sharp tongue, do you hear
me?" Fortunately, she did not choose to respond that way.

Once Judy realized that Josh's caustic words were a spin-off from
his frustration with Courtney, she was able to tie his hurt to how he had
spoken to her: "I understand that Courtney has been giving you mixed
signals lately and that she turned you down for the Friday night social.
That helps me understand why you spoke in a moody way. What's the
latest?"

Josh was not skilled at talking in depth about his feelings, but he did disclose that it didn't make sense that Courtney was so hard to read. Judy replied wisely to her son: "Josh, I know there will be plenty more of those kinds of frustrations in the months and years ahead. Rather than just acting angrily toward me when you've been hurt by someone else, I'd like you to feel free to tell me what's eating away at you. Let's discuss ways you can handle your hurts so they don't come out as anger toward me or some other innocent bystander."

With that lead-in, they were able to talk about how they could keep him from displacing anger. Josh was learning that his mother was willing to hear his needs, meaning he had an ally in moments of despair.

Once you recognize that your children's anger has originated in other circumstances, you can follow Judy's lead by discussing options with your youngster. How would this create a different form of communication in your home? (For instance, "When my daughter is upset because of rejection from her peers, I don't need to be so thin-skinned that I express hurt when she talks rudely to me. I need to slow down in order to get a better understanding of her day's stresses, and then sift through her options with her," or "My son feels pressure to be the best in his sports activities, and I could talk with him about ways to handle the emotions this generates.")

_____

_____

_____

Let's shift gears and recognize that sometimes angry parent-child exchanges are caused by the parents' inability to resolve their outside relationship pains. A parent, for instance, can displace anger toward the child when:

- The marriage relationship is in distress and problems are hanging in the air
- Work pressures cause you to go home with a spirit of pessimism
- You are having tension with members of the extended family
- A friend has been irresponsible or unreliable
- A divorce is pending, or there are strains with an ex-spouse

- Too many people outside the family are vying for time that would otherwise be spent at home

What outside relationship strains cause you to unleash anger unnecessarily toward your children? (For instance, "My spouse and I disagree often, and it puts me in a bad mood which then is displayed with my children," or "I have friends who want so much of my time that I feel stressed when I'm required to address my kids' needs.")

_____

_____

_____

Why do you choose to unload your frustration onto your children? (For instance, "I can never get my mother to understand anything I have to say, so it seems that my kids just happen to be the ones it's easiest for me to vent on," or "My son's argumentative nature reminds me of my husband's stubbornness, and I can't tolerate the thought that he would grow up with the same insensitivity toward women.")

_____

_____

_____

Dr. Carter spoke with Judy about the pessimism that often accompanied her discussions with Josh. She admitted: "He reminds me of my brother, who was always so belligerent when we were growing up. I can't stand it when I see him being so mean to his sister because it reminds me of the pain I had to endure in my original family."

"It's fair that you would want to teach your son to have greater respect for his sister than your brother had for you," the doctor acknowledged. "I'm wondering if the intensity of your anger toward Josh is being influenced by the fact that you may not have come to terms with your long-standing pain." This sparked a long and productive discussion with Judy about the need to separate Josh from feelings she harbored that had nothing to do with her son.

Keep in mind that a main purpose of anger is to stand up for the need to feel respected. If you have not felt respected by significant people in your life, the simplest display of disrespect from your children can set off anger that is raw and near the surface. Are you willing to recognize that your displacement of anger toward your kids is a choice you are making that can be channeled in a more appropriate direction?

To improve your ability to see where you tend to displace your anger toward your children, first list three or four of the frustrating circumstances in your life that do not include your kids. (For instance, "The ongoing breakdown in communication with my spouse," or "My lack of fulfillment due to friends who have not been there for me in times of need.")

_____

_____

_____

Now go back through each of these items of unfinished anger and make note of how it might be displayed in misapplied anger toward one of your children. (For instance, "When my spouse and I have had an argument, I give my children the cold shoulder," or "In my loneliness due to feeling abandoned by my friend, I put extra pressure on my child to be very supportive of my feelings.")

_____

_____

_____

Let's do the same exercise in relation to how your children may display unfinished anger toward you. What are three or four of the most common relationship problems in your children's lives that seem to keep them on an emotional edge? (For instance, "My daughter is in constant contact with a girl who is very domineering over her," or "My son's coach is a hard driver who demands ultimate loyalty.")

_____

_____

_____

Now reexamine each of these trouble spots to determine how it negatively affects the home atmosphere. (For instance, "My daughter is hypersensitive to any hint of invalidation," or "My son feels so criticized by his coach that it creates insecurities in the way he responds at home.")

_____

_____

_____

As you are able to see the connection between outside frustration and the anger inside the home, you can make the necessary adjustments so family members are allies with one another instead of antagonists. Judy recognized that she tended to be more tense toward Josh and Amanda after she had a frustrating experience with one of her customers. Recognizing the unfairness of displacing that frustration onto them, she determined to create a form of accountability for herself. She could tell the children, "I want you to be aware that this has not been a good day for me, so if I seem out of it, don't be shocked. In the meantime, I'll be careful not to put my burdens unfairly on you."

Likewise, Judy became more adept at reading her children's moods for the purpose of determining if there was really something else pushing their anger along. If Josh was especially moody, she might say: "I remember you saying a little earlier that you had a rough exchange with your algebra teacher. Is that part of the frustration that you're carrying right now?"

By identifying outside hurts, the family learned not to draw each other into the anger that belonged elsewhere. In what common circumstances can your family do the same? (For instance, "If I've had tension with my spouse, I can let my son know that this is not a good time for us to discuss his weekend plans; I can get back with him in an hour," or "I can be sensitive enough to realize that my daughter may have lots of things on her mind when she gets home from school, so if she's moody, instead of reacting harshly I can slow down and ask her to talk to me about the day's frustrations.")

_____

_____

_____

Personal Failures

In the same way that relationship strains can cause anger to be displaced among parents and children, personal failures can create the possibility of misguided communication. Failure breeds emotional duress that can very quickly turn into anger if it is not readily resolved. For instance:

• In Judy's work as an interior designer, many of her customers were pleased with her work, but she also worked with some people who seemed impossible to please. Whenever she had to field their complaints, it easily created deflated feelings and she would wonder why she couldn't always measure up.

• Josh had a history of being a good student, but as he got promoted into the higher grades he found the demands of school to be overwhelming at times. He was increasingly frustrated that the highest grades did not come his way as they had in the past.

• Amanda thoroughly enjoyed her social activities, but she had difficulty coming to terms with the cliques that were so common among preteen girls. She often felt upset because of the petty rejection from some peers.

If failures are frequent or powerful, they can negatively affect the home atmosphere. What failures have you experienced that create a negative impact on your family relations? (For instance, "I recently had a falling out with a close friend, and it's caused me to be more moody than normal," or "Things are not going well at work, and my tension shows when I'm at home.")

_____

_____

_____

How about your children? What failures have they experienced that creates increased tension at home? (For instance, "My daughter failed in her tryout for a solo in her choir's musical presentation, and she felt humiliated," or "My son worked hard on a science project, but could only get a C for his efforts.")

_____

_____

_____

When you or your kids are struggling in the aftermath of failure, how does it affect the mood of anger? (For instance, "I know I'm grouchy when things aren't going well at my job," or "My daughter has a 'leave-me-alone' attitude when she's experienced a loss or a disappointment.")

_____

_____

_____

Dr. Carter explained to Judy: "Many times when anger is expressed between parent and child, the matter at hand is not really the issue. You may argue, for example, about schedule conflicts, but the argumentative tone is the result of hurt that originates from another source."

"Boy, is that ever true," Judy responded. "Both Josh and Amanda can be edgy about something that's gone wrong, and before you know it, they respond to a simple statement from me with unnecessary emotional energy. It drives me nuts!"

"When that happens, your challenge is to stay objective and not be unduly influenced by their outside strain," replied the doctor. "For instance, if Josh snaps at you when you've barely given him a reason to be irritable, that's a strong indication that something else is eating away at his insides. Your task will be to sidestep the temptation to snap back at him and to probe instead for the deeper reason for his moodiness."

Not long after this conversation with the doctor, Judy did indeed have a chance to practice what they had discussed. She asked Josh to bring his dirty clothes to the laundry room, and Josh shouted, "Why can't you just leave me alone? I'm tired of having to stop everything I'm doing just so I can do more chores!"

In the past, Judy would have responded to this irrational remark as if it were an invitation to fight. But this time she paused and gently said: "Josh, I'm guessing something must be bothering you right now.

I'll still need you to get your dirty clothes for me, but before you do, maybe we can talk about your day." Within a few minutes she learned that he had been demoted from the starting line-up on his basketball team and that the coach had expressed disappointment in his play. Her reply was: "I guess that explains why you seemed so irritated. You're probably not in the mood to be told what to do by an adult." At that point, she still held firmly to her original request, but she was able to talk with Josh about alternative ways to reveal his troubled feelings.

When you recognize that your children's anger is linked to personal failures, how can you respond in a way that eases the tension? (For instance, "I could refrain from defending myself, and instead I could talk with my daughter about her hurt feelings," or "I could speak calmly about the need for my son to fill me in each day about the disappointments he's dealing with.")

_____

_____

_____

Once you put your focus on the origin of the displaced anger, your discussion can be much more productive and relevant.

For Family Discussion

1. When we unload anger onto family members, there are often outside factors pushing the anger along. What outside frustrations cause each of you to take out your anger in the home? Discuss this one person at a time.

2. Keeping a good balance in time commitments can be crucial to minimizing anger. Let each person discuss how he or she can do a better job of managing time.

3. When outside relationships create frustration, it can affect the mood in your home relationships. How can you determine as a family to

be supportive of one another when each of you has frustrations with those outside the home?

4. When you have failed or experienced disappointment, you might be inclined to be moody at home. What failures or disappointments cause each of you to become annoyed around the house?

5. When it is clear that one of you is feeling angry because of outside strain, what is the best way to keep it from ruining family communications?

For Further Reflection

Psalm 116:6–7 reminds us: "The Lord preserves the simple. . . . Return to your rest, oh my soul, for the Lord has dealt bountifully with you."

1. What keeps your family life from being simple? What compels you or your children to overload life? How does this affect you emotionally?

2. What benefits would your family experience if you had more time together to play, laugh, or enjoy each other's company? How can you rearrange priorities to help this happen?

Proverbs 2:20 says: "Walk in the way of good men and keep the paths of the righteous."

3. When you have too many stressors, how is your spiritual life depleted? How might your anger or frustration with your kids represent displaced anger that is due to unresolved stress?

In Matthew 5:23–24, Jesus taught: "If therefore you are presenting yourself at the altar, and there remember that your brother has something against you, leave your offering there before the altar, and go your way; first be reconciled to your brother."

4. Loose ends in one relationship can create problems when pursing other activities. When has tension with your kids been spurred on by

unresolved conflict elsewhere? How can anger be minimized by first coming to terms with those outside relationship problems? Why do some people procrastinate when they need to address outside relationship stressors?

As recorded in Matthew 11:28, Jesus invites us to Himself: "Come to me all who are weary and heavy-laden, and I will give you rest."

5. What is the rest that is offered to us by Jesus? Why do we sometimes forget to make him our place of refuge?

6. Sometimes parents act out their frustration toward their children because they have not come to terms with personal failure. What is it about this problem that keeps anger unnecessarily alive? As you learn to live in the mercy provided by Christ, how does this help bring healing into your emotional exchanges with your children?

12

THE OVERCOMER'S MIND-SET

STEP 12: Set aside an attitude of defeat, and recognize that in each situation you can choose to be an overcomer.

One of the most agonizing passages of Scripture is Romans 7:14–24. The apostle Paul describes how he has within himself the wish to do what is right, only to find that he does the very thing he knows not to do. He describes it as a battle between his sinful side and the spiritual person he wants to be. In verse 24 he concludes, "Oh wretched man that I am!" Despite his best efforts, he can't find permanent victory on his own strength over his wrong impulses.

He was speaking in general terms, but his words could certainly be applied to parents who have good ideas about how to act at home, only to allow themselves to display the very traits they have promised themselves they would not continue.

It is not at all uncommon for us to hear parents conclude, "I know what I'm supposed to do at home, but somehow it just doesn't happen the way I map it out in my mind." Then, in words similar to Paul's anguishing cry, they say, "This is just not going to work!"

As professionals who have devoted our entire careers to solving people problems, we are not inclined to receive such declarations well. We believe that some circumstances present greater challenges than others.

We even believe that some families are so firmly entrenched in maladaptive patterns that they seemingly defy all logic and reason. But we refuse to believe that anyone who wants to be emotionally balanced can reach such a desperate position that he or she has no option but to collapse in complete defeat. Sometimes relationships fail to meet their potential, but individuals who want to grow can still thrive despite relationship disappointment.

When reading Paul's agonizing words in Romans 7, it is best to continue reading to discover what he has to say in chapter eight. Despite his feelings of despair, he reminds us that we can be overcomers if we live consistently in the strength provided by God (see Romans 8:31–37). So it can be with moms and dads.

Kimberly was the mother of three boys, age nineteen, fourteen, and twelve. The oldest son, Sammy, lived away from the house and made a series of choices that were sure to end in disaster, barring a major turn around. He developed a habit of using illicit drugs. He had a bad temper and a history of troubled relations. In short, he was a severe disappointment to his parents and to anyone who tried to help him succeed.

Kimberly's focus in counseling was to learn how to address discipline issues with her other two sons so they would not meet the same fate as their older brother. Dr. Minirth had treated one for attention deficit disorder, and once a medicinal approach was implemented the family had reason to feel optimistic. But whenever the doctor spoke with Kimberly, it was obvious that she had difficulty in maintaining an upbeat spirit.

In one conversation, Dr. Minirth remarked to her: "Kimberly, you seem discouraged even though your son has shown great improvement in his level of concentration and cooperation." Indeed, Jeremy, the fourteen year old, was making great efforts to be more attentive, and his anger was not as prominent as before.

Heaving a huge sigh, Kimberly replied, "Well, I know Jeremy is trying to cooperate, but there's still so much to address." Adding another sigh, she said, "He and his younger brother will still bicker over every little thing, and I swear they're going to wear me out before they both get old enough to move out on their own. I don't know if I can handle having two teenagers at once."

Kimberly had experienced so much stress with Sammy that she instinctively began to look for the worst in the other two boys, Jeremy and Michael. Using a style of reasoning called generalization, she would remember difficulties experienced with the oldest son and assume that the other two would have similar tendencies.

When anger has been a distasteful part of your life, it can be easy to accept broad negative assumptions as certainty. For instance, if a child was headstrong as a grade school child, parents might generalize and assume, "This child is sure to give me fits in the teen years." Or perhaps if a child has told lies in the past, the assumption might be made that she can never be trusted again.

The Mind of Defeat

Such thinking is part of a larger problem that we call the mind of defeat. This is typified by assuming a stance of pessimism before a negative occurrence even materializes. The mind of defeat is definitely common in angry families, since the anger erodes feelings of confidence and prompts family members to be chronically on guard.

When might you be prone to make negative assumptions about your child, even though the immediate evidence does not yet indicate a need to be pessimistic? (For instance, "I have accused my daughter of wrong behavior before taking time out to gather the facts," or "When I need to get cooperation from my son, I assume that he won't cooperate before I ever approach him with the issue.")

_____

_____

_____

When do your children nurse false or pessimistic assumptions about you even though you have not done anything out of line? (For instance, "My daughter is defensive when she senses that I'm going to ask for her help," or "My son rolls his eyes when I simply say that I need to talk with him about something.")

_____

_____

_____

Ultimately, it is not the behavior of other people that creates anger within yourself. How you mediate upon their behavior is the final factor determining your emotional path. Defeated people are so prone to interpreting events with futility that tension and emotional collapse are a virtual certainty. A feeling of hopelessness can become so pervasive that efforts to address conflict only feed the prevailing assumption that failure will occur.

To get an idea of whether you sometimes fall prey to the mind of defeat, check these statements and see which might apply to you fairly often. You may also want to write the initials of other family members who would relate to those statements.

_____ I feel tense when others do not give credibility to my way of thinking.

_____ There are times when I nurse the thought, *I can't believe I have to put up with this.*

_____ I get hung up on the lack of fairness or logic in my relationships.

_____ When others persist in insensitivity, I might hold onto an ongoing sour attitude.

_____ I have had moments of giving up on hope.

_____ I can't seem to deal with people who are unwilling to change.

_____ Cynicism or resentment are traits that follow me too often.

_____ Although evidence may indicate that another person won't cooperate, that doesn't stop me from arguing or pleading my case.

_____ I let the problems and inconsistencies of others weigh me down.

_____ I find it difficult to accept that others avoid dealing with their obvious dysfunctions.

We each know moments of frustration as we encounter people who are chronically difficult, so it would be highly unusual if you did not relate to any of the statements. If you checked five or more, be aware that you could lapse easily into a defeatist mind-set, which keeps you susceptible to debilitating anger.

When you allow defeat to have a stronghold in your anger, it is likely that there are three factors that keep you caught in your poor responses to conflict: (1) unwillingness to accept conflict, (2) a sense of no choices, and (3) a demand for fairness. Let's look at each of these factors separately.

Unwillingness to Accept Conflict

Jeremiah 17:9 offers this unflattering caricature of human nature: "The heart of man is deceitful above all things and is desperately wicked; who can understand it?" Problems and conflict are a permanent part of life. No matter how wise or appropriate you may be in your dealings with others, it is predictable that others will have problems that clash with your own problematic traits. No amount of coordination or positive communication can ensure that you will become perfectly blended with another person. Differentness is a certainty. Couple that with the truth that each person is capable of being insensitive or on a separate wave length, and we can easily assume that every relationship has the potential for numerous incidents of discord.

Despite the logic of this reasoning, some individuals nonetheless press forward with an agenda of creating total harmony. Once the harmony does not materialize, anger is experienced as the person assumes that personal composure cannot be found until the ideal balance is met. Little or no allowance is made for the truth that discord happens.

The simplest way to determine that a person cannot accept conflict is to listen for key phrases that reveal the deeper mind-set:

"I can't believe you . . ."
"Why in the world do you . . ."
"If only you would . . ."
"It seems to me that . . ."
"Why can't you just . . ."

When do you find yourself making statements that reveal you are having a hard time accepting conflict? (For instance, "I repeatedly speak to my daughter in an incredulous tone of voice, as I ask her why she made the decisions she makes," or "I become impatient when I correct my son over a problem we've discussed many times, as if he's supposed to agree with me whenever I utter an opinion.")

_____

_____

_____

Kimberly learned that a mind-set of defeat was behind her chronic words of frustration as she spoke with her sons about discipline matters. She often asked rhetorical questions: "What's it going to take to make you cooperate?" or "What is wrong with you; why do you act that way?" When asking such questions, she was not attempting to gather useful information. Rather, her questions were an exasperated way of showing that she was straining to accept their imperfections.

What imperfections in your children do you find difficult to accept? (For instance, "I cannot accept that my son thinks his rock star idols are good role models," or "I find it hard to accept that my daughter feels so free to speak condescendingly to me.")

_____

_____

_____

People like Kimberly set themselves up to feel defeated because their ideal standards leave little or no room for failure and disappointment. They choose not to accept the truth that their children can and will veer off course, sometimes disastrously so. Make no mistake, we are not proponents of mediocre standards. We believe it is wise to uphold strong values in the home. We do point out to parents, though, that they will nurse excessive anger if they convince themselves they cannot accept the reality that their children can be emotionally frail.

Even as you continue to uphold discipline and values, what conflicts with your children could you choose to accept? (For instance, "I can accept the fact that when my daughter says she hates me, she's hurting at that moment, and I could adjust my comments to address the hurt," or "I can continue to keep my reasonable standards for my son's curfew, even as I accept that he may think he knows better than me.")

_____

_____

_____

Dr. Minirth challenged Kimberly to get a more realistic grip on her family life: "Can you see that your anger would diminish greatly if you accepted the truth that Jeremy can be moody and sometimes harsh in the way he treats you or his brother? I'm not saying that you should cease from teaching good values or from applying consequences. I'm saying that when you cease being shocked by this reality, you are positioned to respond to him more rationally."

"That's going to be hard," she admitted, "because I have such high aspirations for him."

"Hold onto those hopes," replied the doctor. "Just keep your assessment of him anchored in truth. Right now, he's an angry youth. That's frustrating, though hopefully it won't always be that way. Despite his emotional confusion, he needs you to stay emotionally sober. That means you'll need to make room for discomfort even as you keep your mind on the better way."

A Sense of No Choices

When parents succumb to a mind of defeat, we commonly hear them describe the feeling of being stuck. For years Kimberly was prone to throwing up her hands and saying, "What difference does it make? Nothing works!" She had read the books, listened to the experts, and concluded that none of the discipline tips would cause her kids to improve. As the tension remained in her home, she began believing she had no options left.

Usually when we talk with parents who feel they are at the end of their rope, we get a history of how emotions and disciplines were addressed in prior years in the home. Because hindsight invariably yields 20/20 vision, we can virtually always spot how conflict was mismanaged. People with a mind of defeat often look back upon their historical hurts and conclude that they are doomed to continue in the pain they have always known. They see past failure as proof that they cannot expect positive change today.

Kimberly typified many when she told Dr. Minirth: "I doubt that you're going to be able to tell me anything new. I've read every article on parenting I could get my hands on and I've tried umpteen different techniques, but most days I still feel like I'm sitting on square one." Presumably, this indicates that Kimberly was fresh out of choices. Right? That was her conclusion!

Dr. Minirth explained to Kimberly: "Even though you feel you've tried everything and run out of choices, there are two thoughts I want you to consider. First, you may need to go back to some of the basics and try them again. Second, I'm going to encourage you to be more patient as you wait for the desired results to surface."

Indeed, part of Kimberly's defeatism stemmed from her tendency to apply a good approach, only to give up on it relatively quickly if it did not pan out as she wished. For instance, she had learned years ago that it was necessary to apply consequences whenever Jeremy threw a temper tantrum. Yet she often said to herself, *Those consequences never work because the next day he'll be just as likely to do the same thing.* The result was many angry exchanges between herself and her son as she would remind him (and reinforce negative expectations) that he was a chronic thorn in her side. It did not dawn on her that she would have to apply patience as she repeatedly chose to continue with wise choices.

When have you felt you were out of choices with your children? (For instance, "I've been lecturing my daughter for years regarding the need to plan ahead, but it never works," or "I've given up talking with my son about smoking cigarettes because he's so bull-headed, he'll do whatever he feels like doing.")

_____

_____

_____

When your kids sense your feeling of hopelessness, what seems to be the response? (For instance, "I think my daughter feels every bit as pessimistic as I do that our relationship will always be tense," or "I think my son feels a sense of victory when he sees that he's worn me out.")

_____

_____

_____

Dr. Minirth explained to Kimberly: "Sometimes it takes weeks or months, or even years, before you have the satisfaction of seeing the results of your parenting efforts. In his stubbornness, Jeremy may make it his goal to make you assume that you can't get through to him. When you are at the point of exasperation, keep in mind that you still have choices."

"Like what?" came her retort. "I don't have anything new to add to what I've already tried."

"Once choice is to quit," said Dr. Minirth. "Another choice is to yell or put him on a guilt trip. Another choice is to tell him how worthless he is." He paused to let her see that these reactions, though lousy options, were indeed true choices. He continued, "Of course you could persist in talking calmly with him about the better path, and you could also continue discussing consequences calmly with him, applying them when necessary. The choice is not new, but this doesn't mean it should be discarded. Sometimes you'll need to keep going back to the basics."

Her reply was predictable: "But consequences don't faze him. If I ground him for a weekend, he's still going to be ornery the next chance he gets."

"At that point, you could continue choosing patience. It may be quite some time before you'll see the desired results; nonetheless, you can conclude that staying your course with a combination of firmness and calmness is the better way."

When parents say they are out of choices, they usually mean, "I haven't gotten the desired results, so I quit." Focus less on the short-term frustration and keep your eye on your long-term parenting goals. Think for a moment: even as your kids continue in wrong behaviors or attitudes, what is right about your persistence in choosing calm, firm consequences? (For instance, "I can let my son know that my love for him is what keeps me from succumbing to his demands that I overlook his poor choices of activities," or "I can show my daughter that I'm patient enough to wait for her to mature so she can finally see the wisdom of my guidance.")

_____

_____

_____

You always have choices as you manage your conflicts at home. You *do not* necessarily have the power to control how your children receive the choices you make. In your moments of disappointment, take care that you do not cease holding to loving and appropriate action.

A Demand for Fairness

Over the years, how many times have you heard your children complain about the lack of fairness in the events before them? Children often gripe about the punishments they receive as they complain that a friend or sibling does not have to suffer so. "That's not fair!" becomes their battle cry. Likewise, they moan about the good fortune of others and they convince themselves that other people have all the good luck while they languish in perpetual misery.

Sound familiar? We adults can quickly (and justly) conclude that the phrase "That's not fair" is one of the whiniest, most immature statements a child can utter.

But before being too hard on these whiny youngsters, let's be willing to put the focus on the parents, who may hold to the same complaint. Most adults, mind you, probably don't complain about unfairness in the same nasal, childlike voice. Nonetheless, we have our own moments of despair when faced with life's many injustices. We complain in slightly more sophisticated ways:

"Why me? Why am I always so unappreciated?"
"What's the deal here? What have I done to deserve this mistreatment?"
"What does it take to get through to you?"

"Are you just trying to make my life miserable? If so, I'd say
you're succeeding!"

"It just doesn't seem right that I try so hard but get so little respect
in return."

In what circumstances do you struggle with the lack of fairness in your
child's responses to you? (For instance, "I can work for hours to help my
son entertain some of his friends and get no thanks in return," or "My
daughter shows no recognition of the many sacrifices I make for her, and
that drives me crazy.")

_____

_____

_____

Dr. Minirth addressed this issue with Kimberly after she complained
about the lack of appreciation Jeremy showed for her efforts to arrange
her schedule to accommodate his needs: "I guess Jeremy has no appreciation for the fact that parenting can often be a thankless task. When
I make special adjustments for him, he seems to respond as if he was
entitled to the royal treatment. When I was his age I'd never display the
attitude of entitlement that he displays toward me. This just isn't right."

The doctor agreed. "An appreciative mind is definitely a sign of maturity," he said. "Apparently Jeremy is not on the same page with you
in that regard." Pausing for a moment, he then reflected: "Let's be careful that your desire for relationship fairness does not result in exaggerated anger. You certainly have a message that he needs to hear, so be
willing to play the role of teacher when that's beneficial. Your task is to
remain even-tempered as you relay the right message to him."

"But I get so frustrated at the injustice of it all that my agitation takes
over," she replied.

Dr. Minirth reminded her: "Your feeling of agitation is not entirely
misplaced. I want you to remember that even then, you still have choices
regarding how you respond to him."

When a child responds to you in unfair ways, you still have choices in
how to address the problem. What do you consider to be the wisest way
to respond to the unfairness of your children's sour attitude or misguided

behavior? (For instance, "When my daughter tells me I've never helped her with her many needs, I could choose to stay out of a defensive reaction even if she doesn't recognize my good efforts," or "When my son complains about the unreasonableness of my boundaries for him, I can talk openly about appropriate options and still be firm in my decision.")

_____

_____

_____

It is predictable that every one of us (adult and child alike) would like to see events unfold in a self-satisfying way. This thinking can ensnare us, though, in ongoing anger if we remain tied to insistence that events should always be fair and good. Rather than expending angry energy when this occurs, let's make room for the reality that fairness may prove elusive, but this does not have to lead to harsh responses of anger.

The Overcomer's Mind-Set

When the apostle Paul wrote the words in Romans 7 describing the agony accompanying his struggle with wrong impulses, he did not collapse in defeat. In fact, Romans 8 is one of the most uplifting passages in all Scripture. He proclaimed:

> We have no condemnation when we are in Christ (verse 1)
> As we set our minds on the spirit we can have life and peace (verse 6)
> We are children of God (verse 14)
> We get to call God "daddy" (verse 15)
> We are promised a future of glory (verse 18)
> We will be delivered from corruption (verse 21)
> The Spirit will pray on our behalf when we have no words to say (verse 26)
> God is for us and no one can come against us (verse 31)
> We are more than conquerors through Christ who loved us (verse 37)
> Nothing can separate us from the love of God (verses 38–39)

Though Paul had to be honest about his own shortcomings, he did not succumb to feelings of defeat because he knew that God would continue to uphold him despite his strain. Do you have that same understanding?

As an alternative to the mind of defeat, develop the mind-set of an overcomer. An overcomer is defined as one who refuses to succumb to defeat when faced with adverse circumstances. While being realistic enough to acknowledge the presence of real hurt or disappointment, these people maintain enough independence of mind that they persist in the goal of being emotionally healthy even in trying times.

Kimberly's challenge was to undergird her own spirit with a mind-set that refused to sink in defeat when her sons would not appreciate her. Dr. Minirth explained: "Sometimes you'll need to be the one who holds onto optimism even though it seems you have no good reason to do so. You can be guided by the belief that the choice to stay steady in your efforts with your sons will someday pay positive dividends."

Through counseling, Kimberly began to learn that negative events did not necessarily have to result in disaster. Dr. Minirth repeatedly encouraged her to view each disappointing circumstance as an opportunity to apply wisdom and purpose. When she complained that it just seemed as if he were preaching a brand of positive thinking, his reply was sure: "Well, I definitely don't want to preach the alternative—defeated thinking!"

In each difficulty with your children, you have a choice to be optimistic or pessimistic. How can your approach to anger management improve if you choose to take a more positive approach in your communication? (For instance, "I'd be less inclined to negatively label my son as a malcontent," or "I'd act on the assumption that I have good things to say to my daughter even if she's not able to appreciate it now.")

_____

_____

_____

To consistently manage your anger with an overcomer's mentality, there are four key insights you need to ponder and incorporate. Let's examine them one by one.

Use Negative Experiences as a Motivation to Be a Much Healthier Person

Kimberly often felt riddled with guilt about having lost her temper too often with her sons. She feared they would never again take her seriously because they knew she'd just become angry whenever they had problems to solve: "How can I maintain any credibility with Jeremy and Michael when they've seen me blow up over things that I should have handled more appropriately?"

Keeping a realistic perspective, Dr. Minirth explained: "You don't need to despair when you make mistakes with your kids. Instead be honest. Let them know that you see your own errors. Talk openly about the better alternatives. They need to see that even with your imperfection, you're still growing and maturing. Let them know that you're committed to hang in with them just as you hope they'll do the same with you."

"That would definitely be a change of pace for us," she admitted. "Usually I feel so guilty after one of our bad spells that I just try to downplay the incident and move on to something else."

"Kids respect adult honesty," Dr. Minirth said. "If you can admit your wrongs and talk about positive choices, you establish credibility and leadership."

How do your children take cues from you once there has been a clear conflict? (For instance, "I can tell that my son's length of healing time is directly tied to the attitude I maintain once we've had a major spat," or "My daughter definitely becomes defensive when she feels that I'm taking too long to snap out of a bad mood.")

_____

_____

_____

How can you establish positive leadership as you indicate that conflict is a time when true learning and growth can occur? (For instance, "I'd be willing to receive input from my daughter when we've disagreed because I want to illustrate that we can develop good listening skills," or "I could talk with my son about the struggles I had at his age and how I understand the needs that he has.")

_____

_____

_____

Growth and improvement rarely occur when things go right. Rather than viewing your strained moments as a sure disaster, look for the learning experience and make it an open matter. Debriefing in the aftermath of conflict can be both healing and educational.

Rather Than Fixating on Past Failure, Focus on Future Possibility

Once you have determined that you are not threatened by current stressors but can grow in spite of them, you are less inclined to obsess about past mistakes. For instance, recall that Kimberly sought treatment because she felt she had failed in how she managed conflict with her oldest son, Sammy. In counseling, she came to realize that when one of her younger boys made mistakes similar to Sammy's, she could quickly put a negative interpretation on it. *Oh no,* she might think. *Here we go again. Looks like I'm going to have to prepare myself for the same old battles I fought with Sammy.*

With guidance, she learned to approach new tensions with a more future-oriented approach. She could entertain a thought such as, "OK, I've been through this type of problem before. As I remember some of the results of past anger episodes, I can choose a different and more reasoned approach. I'm determined to respond more confidently."

In most cases, our failed experience of anger follows a fairly predictable pattern. For instance, Kimberly was the type of person who would reflexively jump onto a negative situation too strongly before she had a chance to think about a better alternative. In her case, she had to learn to slow down her response, speaking differently to herself when tension arose: "OK, I don't like what my son is doing now, but instead of giving an impulsive response let's see how a more reasoned approach will help." It was a great step forward for her when she recognized she could use her past miscues to motivate her toward current and future adjustments.

What about you? Surely you can identify trends when you have mis-managed conflict with your kids in the past. What tendencies do you see in yourself? (For instance, "I tend to hold in my frustration until I can stand it no more, then I explode," or "I tend to accuse too quickly without patiently gathering facts.")

_____

_____

_____

As you identify past mistakes, what current and future adjustments can you make as a result of your awareness? (For instance, "I need to speak more immediately to our differences so I won't let emotional energy carry me away," or "I need to be a much more thorough listener instead of popping off when I first feel ticked.")

_____

_____

_____

Pick Your Battles Carefully Because of Your Goal to Be Healthy

Overcomers choose not to become bogged down in fruitless battles. Realizing the need to love and accept their kids' imperfection, they choose instead to save expressions of firmness for moments that really matter. For instance, Kimberly recognized that she did not have to play referee every time Jeremy and Michael bickered. Likewise, she did not have to respond in a huff when Jeremy complained about her differing priorities.

This attitude is a contrast to the defeatists' tendency to view negatives as ongoing proof that life cannot be expected to offer anything other than tension. Overcoming parents realize that their children's maturation (as well as their own) is a process. It does not happen overnight, yet it will happen. That being the case, they can choose acceptance over judgment, patience over insistence, and forgiveness over begrudging.

Focus on the incidents when you become angry with your children. If you are like most, the possible anger-producing circumstances are many. Now, think of the impact you would have on your children's emotional health if you chose to spotlight each and every potential conflict. The results would be devastating!

What tends to happen in your home when you focus too intently on your child's negatives? (For instance, "My daughter resorts to broad characterizations by accusing me of always being unfair or never caring about her boyfriend," or "My son becomes so numb to my complaints that he successfully tunes me out.")

_____

_____

_____

Now contrast the overemphasis on conflict by considering the possibility of being cautious and judicious about entering into conflict. How is the home atmosphere improved when you choose to be more moderate in talking about the things that create anger? (For instance, "It allows me the chance to focus more openly on what I do like about my son," or "I can illustrate that I see my role more as an encourager than an enforcer.")

_____

_____

_____

As you develop an overcomer's mind-set, continue in your willingness to communicate about the frustrating circumstances that warrant your attention, but do so with the broader goal of being known for fair-mindedness and love.

Draw upon Internal, Not External, Strength

Whereas defeatists assume they can only be strong if the outer world cooperates, overcomers operate with a more internal base of strength. They are wise enough to realize that problems will ever be upon us. That is, no family is without conflict, no teenager is perfectly synchronized with parents, and no parent is ideal in managing discipline. Accepting these truths, overcomers know better than to place their emotional well-being into the fickle circumstances of the outer world.

Through counseling, Kimberly came to recognize that her anger was too easily swayed by the unpredictable moods of her sons. Once she recognized that she would not fall apart each time her sons erred or differed, she was able to plan her response to their moods by consulting her inner sense of right and wrong. For instance, she was particularly perturbed one afternoon when she received notice that Jeremy had received a detention after verbally sparring with a teacher at school. In the past, she would have quickly scolded him, adding to the tension of the situation by lecturing with great agitation. This time, however, she took another approach: "I'll still need to talk with Jeremy about this problem, but it is important for me to show him how a mature, composed adult handles adversity. I know that my emotional demeanor is the best teaching device that I have to offer at a time like this."

As an overcomer, Kimberly was learning that her family could choose to respond to tense circumstances without belittling anger. She realized that her sons would not necessarily change right away, but she trusted that a less volatile means of responding to anger would set a positive tone for the years to come. She recognized that her own modeling of inward strength would be her best teaching method.

In what circumstances will you need to draw less upon external circumstances and more upon your inner strength and integrity? (For instance, "When my son becomes insulting or biting in his choice of words, I want to illustrate the more respectful alternative," or "When my kids are argumentative, I need to live with the resolve to be steady in my demeanor.")

_____

_____

_____

How do you need to adjust your priorities to be less affected by externals and more reliant on your internal strength? (For instance, "It helps when I consistently give myself some quiet time each day to meditate and become focused on my highest priorities," or "I need to trim the family schedule so we are not so torn by many obligations.")

_____

_____

_____

_____

No parent is able to guide his or her children into the young adult years without some frustrations and mishaps along the way. It is not reasonable to establish a goal of anger-free living. It is reasonable, however, to determine that in your anger you can continue being a respectful leader, willing to set the pace for constructive communications.

❧ ❧

For Family Discussion

1. Have each family member discuss moments when he or she feels most defeated and exasperated. What is it that you wish the others could understand about you during those times?

2. Have each person identify common family conflicts. Specifically, what are some of the quirks or imperfections in your family unit that each of you may need to accept as ongoing fact?

3. Discuss your opinions about this thought: "It is impossible to control your anger when you are faced with unfair circumstances."

4. What gives you hope that your family can look forward to a future of satisfaction and family harmony? Have each person respond to this.

5. How can you draw upon past disappointment or failure to make you stronger as individuals and stronger as a family unit?

6. By recognizing that none of us is perfect, it makes sense that we should not try to find strength solely from each other's behavior. Have each person describe how he or she can be inwardly strong even when the circumstances are frustrating.

For Further Reflection

Psalm 42:3 records the agonizing words: "My tears have been my food day and night, while they say to me all day long, 'Where is your God?'"

1. When have you experienced times of great personal defeat? What affect does this have on your ability to manage conflict with your children?

2. Your kids look to you for motivation. When they see you in a state of defeat, how do they react? How can you tell when your downtrodden feelings become their downtrodden feelings?

In Psalm 44:9, David speaks dejectedly to God: "Yet Thou hast rejected us and brought us to dishonor."

3. When might you feel tempted to blame God for your woes? How does this feed an attitude of victimization? How does this affect your management of anger?

Psalm 42:5 records the words: "Hope in God for I shall again praise Him for the help of His presence."

4. What does it mean to turn over our despair and place our hope in God? Specifically, in what circumstances do we need to trust God's guidance more fully? How does this impact your own emotional disposition when you are with your children?

Romans 8:6 tells us: "For the mind set on the flesh is death, but the mind set on the Spirit is life and peace."

5. What does it mean to set your mind on the Spirit, specifically as this relates to your role as a parent? How can you expect your children to respond if you illustrate that you are able to draw peace from God?

6. Suppose your children are unimpressed with your efforts to draw strength from God. How might this send you back into a pattern of defeat? How can you keep this from derailing you in your efforts to be emotionally balanced?

APPENDIX

ANGER, TEENAGERS, AND MEDICATION

It is quite common for parents to question the physiological dimension of their children's emotional struggles. Naturally, they wonder if and when medicines should be used. Indeed, anger can have a medical dimension. The physiological parameter in bipolar disorder, major depressive disorder, attention-deficit hyperactivity disorder (ADHD), paranoid schizophrenia, and posttraumatic stress disorder (PTSD) is examined in this Appendix. In most cases, anger can be a normative part of the teen years, and it can certainly be exaggerated by these disorders.

Today research is steeped with studies tracing the genetic and physiological dimension. For example, identical twins raised in the same home are concurrent for bipolar disorder 66–96 percent of the time if the disorder exists in one. They are concurrent for the disorder 75 percent of the time even if raised separately. Also, if one identical twin has major depressive disorder, the other twin has the disorder 60–76 percent of the time. They are concurrent for the disorder 44–67 percent of the time if raised separately. Furthermore, if one parent has schizophrenia, 10 percent of the children will have the disorder, but the risk jumps to

50 percent if two parents have the disorder. The concordance rate for schizophrenia is 10 percent for nonidentical twins, but 80–90 percent for identical twins. In addition, individuals with obsessive-compulsive disorder have a first-degree relative with OCD 40 percent of the time, individuals with ADHD 35 percent of the time.

It is a simple fact that a physiological dimension exists, though it does not negate or nullify environmental and choice factors. For the genetic and physiological dimension to manifest, an environmental factor usually also has to be present. The environmental factor in adolescence can be medical disease, a virus, a toxin, an injury, drug abuse, peer influence, hormones, poor choices, family anger problems, or just plain stress.

While genetic studies provide almost irrefutable evidence of a physiological dimension, perhaps even more convincing are PET (positron emission tomography) scans that clearly reveal the physiological dimension. These scans are not yet diagnostic, but the evidence is strong indeed. PET scans show glucose uptake, and since the brain functions by glucose uptake the scans reveal abnormal functional patterns in various disorders. Also, just as PET scans reveal abnormal patterns in different disorders of adolescence, MRIs (magnetic resonance imaging) do so as well through neuroimaging studies demonstrating structural or anatomical abnormalities.

To summarize, certain mental disorders in their early stages have both genetic and environmentally mediated factors resulting in structural and functional brain abnormalities that can concretely be seen today through PET scans and MRIs. Furthermore, medications are often effective in treating these disorders since a physiological dimension does exist. These mental issues are analogous to other medical conditions. Just as one would not say to a person with heart disease and angina "Let's only work on your anger," one should not ignore the wonderful medical tools that are available today when a physiological dimension exists in some cases of anger. From extensive research, anger seems to be a factor many times in those prone to heart disease and angina, yet we always treat the coexisting physiological condition. Likewise, we should employ the use of many wonderful medicines today that can decrease inappropriate anger, which has a physiological dimension in its makeup.

Although concrete PET scans and MRIs cannot fully solve the complexity of the physiological dimension, a variety of tests can also yield clarifying data. Individuals with such disorders often demonstrate on PET scans and neuropsychological tests abnormalities in the frontal lobes of the cortex. This is relevant because the frontal lobes control executive functions: response inhibition (anger control), attention control, cognitive flexibility, working memory, and abstract reasoning. Other areas of the brain such as the basal ganglia, thalamus, hypothalamus, amygdala, reticular activating system, and the neural connections between them may also be involved in addition to the frontal lobes. Several studies have demonstrated impaired performance in executive functioning of the frontal lobes, notably the Wisconsin Card Sorting Test (WCST) and Trail Making Test (TMT). The trouble in function is real and functionally documented. This means that it is wise to incorporate the genetic and physiological dimension with the psychological and spiritual dimensions. One dimension does not eliminate the need to consider the others.

In this Appendix are discussions of bipolar disorder, major depressive disorder, ADHD, paranoid schizophrenia, and PTSD; how anger may be one of the presenting symptoms in each; and how medications can address the neurological and psychological dimensions. We should note that the anger in these disorders is different from the common anger seen with separation-individuation conflicts in teenagers, family anger issues, routine reactive anger, and adjustment issues with angry emotions. We should also note that this information is given so that clients can more knowledgeably discuss these disorders with their medical doctor. The information is not given for individuals to make their own diagnosis. A professional is needed since one could overread the information.

Bipolar Disorder

Bipolar disorder is characterized by going from high to low. When high, these people have elevated mood or angry mood, grandiosity, a decreased need for sleep, talkativeness, racing thoughts, distractibility, increased activity, and poor judgment. When low they have feelings of sadness, melancholia, loss of pleasure, guilt, low energy, disturbed sleep, feelings of worthlessness, indecisiveness, and not wanting to live. Anger can be a prominent symptom. Teens with bipolar disorder may have rages. With high or irritable mood, individuals with bipolar disorder have characteristic bright spots. Also, MRIs of those with bipolar disorder reveal subcortical hyperintensities. These findings show complex specificity in neurophysiological and neuroanatomical activities underlying emotions such as anger.

The medical dimension of bipolar disorder is also documented by the myriad beneficial responses of mood stabilizing and anti-anger medications. In 1949 John Cade of Australia discovered that a naturally occurring salt and metal, lithium carbonate, had mood stabilizing and anti-anger effects. Lithium was like a miracle to many angry, manic individuals and their families. However, it had a narrow therapeutic index and safety proved a concern. In the 1960s, medical doctors started using Depakote, an anticonvulsant, off-label in bipolar anger. It worked and introduced the concept that anticonvulsants may stabilize not only seizures but also mania with extremely high mood and anger as well. Most of the anticonvulsants increase an inhibitory amino acid, GABA (gamma-aminobutyric acid) and decrease an excitatory amino acid, glutamate. Thus, they stabilize and often decrease anger. In the 1970s Tegretol, another anticonvulsant, was used off-label for bipolar disorder. The 1990s saw the introduction of several more anticonvulsants (Neurontin, Topamax, Trileptal, and Lamictal) used off-label in bipolar disorder. Lamictal was recently approved along with Lithium for maintenance treatment of bipolar disorder. The newer anticonvulsants do not require blood level testing, and some (Zonegran and Topamax) may even cause weight loss and thus are appreciated more by teenage females who are weight conscious. We would be remiss if we did not mention that the new neuroleptics (Zyprexa, Risperdol, Seroquel, and Geodon) have also been used on-label (Zyprexa) and off-label (Risperdol, Seroquel, and Geodon) in acute manic episodes.

Major Depressive Disorder

Major depressive disorder is characterized by a significant depressed mood for more than two weeks. It is also characterized by irritability or anger. Other symptoms include loss of interest and pleasure, weight changes, changes in sleep patterns, fatigue, feelings of worthlessness, inappropriate guilt, impaired concentration, and recurrent thoughts of death. Finally, agitation is often a prominent feature. Teens who are depressed often appear chronically frustrated.

PET scans of the brain of depressed individuals are dark in general. This indicates that the brain is not functioning well and correspondingly the individual feels melancholic, negative, and angry. Also, studies using the WCST, TMT, and verbal fluency reveal executive functioning deficits. Life may be difficult, though not as difficult as they perceive. There is electrophysiological overactivation in the right hemisphere of unipolar depressed individuals with resulting social-emotional problems such as undue anger.

In the 1950s, while searching for a new antipsychotic medication, a tricyclic antidepressant was found. Also, while searching for a new TB medication, the MAOI antidepressants were discovered. In the 1980s, a new group of medications that focused mostly on one biogenic amine, serotonin, were made; and the world shook with the news of Prozac. Other serotonin antidepressants would follow: Zoloft, Luvox, Paxil, Celexa, and Lexapro. The 1990s saw the birth of new atypical antidepressants: Serzone, Remeron, and Effexor. Because the drugs were more specific, side effects were less. These drugs are commonly used off-label in depressed teens, with many reporting a lifting of mood and a decreasing of anger.

ADHD

ADHD is characterized by such symptoms as not paying attention to details, making careless mistakes, not seeming to listen, being forgetful, difficulty getting organized, being easily distracted, fidgeting, having difficulty remaining seated, being on the go, talking excessively, being impulsive, having difficulty waiting one's turn, and interrupting. Because of their inattention, hyperactivity, and impulsivity the patients are not only prone to quick anger but often arouse anger in family members.

PET scans of these individuals reveal that they are not taking up glucose in the attention centers of the brain. The brain regions controlling inhibition of responses to internal and external stimuli are clearly not functioning normally. On neuropsychological tests such as WCST, young people with ADHD consistently reveal problems on tests of executive functioning. On the Stroop Color-Word test, young people with ADHD consistently have difficulty inhibiting responses to irrelevant stimuli. Porteus Mazes tests reveal the difficulty the ADHD individual has with planning, anticipating, and remembering. Thus the ADHD individual has impairment in cognitive flexibility and the ability to regulate behavior using feedback from the environment. No wonder anger may be an issue, not just physiologically but also psychologically.

Abnormalities are noted on PET scans and neuropsychological tests and also on MRIs. Abnormalities of the prefrontal cortex and basal ganglia are consistently seen on MRIs.

There is a common misconception that ADHD is overdiagnosed. The truth is quite the contrary in general. Unfortunately, with such faulty reasoning these children have been maligned for years and considered underdisciplined and in need of castigation. Without appropriate medical help, many become discouraged and some turn to all kinds of rebellious behavior. This is a proven neurological disorder. Incidentally, research shows that future drug abuse is much higher in those not treated than in those treated.

Medications for ADHD in teens can produce dramatic results. These drugs work by increasing one or two neurotransmitters of the brain. The neurotransmitters are dopamine, which increases attention, and norepinephrine, which decreases the distractibility of the brain. They may work in multiple ways as the amphetamine Adderall does, in several ways as the stimulant methylphenidate (Ritalin, Focalin, Concerta, Metadate, and Methylin) does, or in a more limited way as the new nonstimulant Strattera does. Dexadrine, Wellbutrin, and Provigil are other drugs used either on-label or off-label for ADHD. When these drugs work, they are as close to a miracle as anything seen in psychiatry. Attention may improve dramatically, distractibility decreases, and anger and behavior problems often lessen for both the teen and the parents.

Of course, the medical treatment does not mitigate the need for behavioral psychotherapy. Both are needed.

Paranoid Schizophrenia

Paranoid schizophrenia is characterized by positive symptoms such as confusion, hallucinations, and angry delusions; and by negative symptoms such as alogia, flat affect, anhedonia, autism, and amotivation. Anger is a common and significant component of the delusions and paranoia.

Paranoid schizophrenia is rare and occurs in less than 1 percent of the population, but it is significant in that it may first manifest during the teen years.

Important PET scan findings include reduced prefrontal metabolism and increased dopamine 2 receptors on the postreceptor site. Neuroimaging studies such as the MRI reveal ventricular enlargement, reduction in thalamus volume, and change in temporal lobe structure. The abnormalities in the frontal lobes, the amygdala-hippocampus complex, and the thalamus probably underlie the problems with attention, executive functioning, memory, and delusions with anger. Individuals with schizophrenia also perform poorly on tests of executive functioning and attention.

In the early 1950s, neuroleptics (Thorazine, Mellaril, Stelazine, Prolixin, Haldol, and Novane) that decreased the uptake of dopamine at dopamine 2 postreceptor sites proved to really help in decreasing delusional anger in paranoid schizophrenia. In the 1990s, new atypical antipsychotics that helped not only in the delusions but also in improved sociability were introduced and tended to have many less side effects. These included

Zyprexa, Risperdol, and Seroquel. In the 2000s, Geodon and Abilify were introduced; they were weight-neutral and perhaps even improved mood. In most cases anger decreased significantly with these medicines.

PTSD

No discussion of the medical dimension would be complete without at least a cursory discussion of posttraumatic stress disorder, since the anatomical and functional damage is so striking. PTSD is characterized by a traumatic event; the reexperiencing of the event; distressing dreams of the event; times of acting as though the event is reoccurring; distress when exposed to situations that resemble the traumatic event; avoiding such situations; inability to remember details of the event; decreased interest in usual activities; feelings of detachment from others; a sense of a foreshortened future; and persisting signs of physiological arousal such as difficulty falling asleep, excessive vigilance, exaggerated startle response, difficulty concentrating, and irritability and anger outbursts.

Teens who have witnessed or experienced acts of family or other violence may be suffering from PTSD. In few conditions does the need for both medical and psychological treatments exist as much as in PTSD. With appropriate medication and psychotherapy the atrophy of the hippocampus begins to rescind and symptoms may decrease.

Medications that have been used in PTSD include the serotonergic antidepressants, periodic use of benzodiazepines, anticonvulsants, propranolol, clonidine, and the neuroleptics.

Symptoms Checklists

For parents who want more symptoms of possible bipolar disorder, major depressive disorder, ADHD, and paranoid schizophrenia, here they are. The official criteria lists here are largely taken from the *Diagnostic and Statistical Manual of Mental Disorders–Fourth Edition (DSM-IV)*. However, this should never replace the clinical judgment of a trained professional.

Hypomanic Symptoms of Bipolar Disorder

0 to 10

1. Elevated mood for a distinct period of time
2. Irritable mood for a distinct period of time
3. Grandiose self-esteem
4. Decreased need for sleep
5. Increased talkativeness
6. Racing thoughts
7. Increased distractibility
8. Increased activity
9. Poor judgment such as increased spending or sexual indiscretions

Manic Scale

On a scale of 0 to 10 grade each one of the above. Do you see a pattern?

Major Depressive Disorder

0 to 10

1. Depressed mood for two weeks
2. Decreased interest and pleasure in activities
3. Changes in weight or appetite
4. Changes in sleep
5. Slowness
6. Agitation
7. Fatigue
8. Worthless feelings
9. Impaired concentration
10. Suicidal feelings or feelings of not wanting to live

Depressive Scale

On a scale of 0 to 10 grade each one of the above. Do you see a pattern?

ADHD Symptoms

0 to 10

1. Decreased attention to details
2. Decreased listening
3. Does not follow instructions
4. Does not finish projects
5. Not organized
6. Loses things
7. Increased distractibility
8. Increased forgetfulness
9. Fidgets
10. Hyperactive
11. Does not remain in seat
12. Loud
13. Restless
14. Increased talkativeness
15. Impulsive
16. Does not await turn
17. Interrupts

ADHD Scale

On a scale of 0 to 10 grade each one of the above. Do you see a pattern?

Paranoid Schizophrenia Symptoms

0 to 10

1. Few words (alogia)
2. Low interests (apathy)
3. Lack of facial expression (affect flattening)
4. Lack of enjoyment of life (anhedonia)
5. In own world (autistic)

6. Strongly sees both sides of many opposite issues (ambivalent)

7. Not social (asocial)

8. Disorganized speech (loose associations)

9. Fidgets

10. Sees things that others do not

11. Feels things that others do not

12. Smells things that others do not

13. Hears things that others do not

14. Feels others are watching

15. Feels others are conspiring against them

16. Feels others are reading their mind

17. Feels others are inserting thoughts into their mind

18. Feels others would persecute them

Paranoid Schizophrenia Scale

On a scale of 0 to 10 grade each one of the above. Do you see a pattern?

PTSD Symptoms

0 to 10

1. A severe traumatic event

2. Reexperiencing of the event

3. Distressing dreams of the event

4. Times of acting as though the event is recurring

5. Distress when exposed to similar situations

6. Avoiding such situations

7. Inability to remember details of the event

8. Decreased interest in usual activities

9. Feelings of detachment from others

10. A sense of a foreshortened future

11. Persisting signs of physiological arousal

12. Difficulty falling or staying asleep

13. Excessive vigilance

14. Exaggerated startle response

15. Difficulty concentrating

16. Anger outbursts and irritability

PTSD Scale
On a scale of 0 to 10 grade each one of the above. Do you see a pattern?

Summary Regarding Anger, Teenagers, and Medication

Anger can have a medical dimension and may respond dramatically to new psychiatric medications. Life and death may hang in the balance, since approximately 15 percent of those with major depression or bipolar disorder may kill themselves. Also, left untreated those with ADHD are much more likely to turn to drug abuse. Finally, left untreated those with paranoid schizophrenia will usually be angry, suspicious, and unable to relate socially to others in a meaningful way, and those with PTSD will live a life of never-ending fear and irritability. Of course, not all anger has a significant medical component, but sometimes it does and this has brought relief to the parents of many teenagers. The bulk of this book deals with the psychological dimension; this Appendix balances that by focusing on the medical. Please refer to this list of various medications for bipolar disorder, major depressive disorder, ADHD, and paranoid schizophrenia.

A List of Psychiatric Medications by Categories of Use

This is a list by category of usage of psychiatric medications. Some are used on-label; others are used off-label, such as some of the anticonvulsants that are used for pain relief and mood stabilization.

Categories of Psychiatric Medications

I. Mood stabilizers

    A. Lithium carbonate (Eskalith, Lithonate, Eskalith CR)

    B. Anticonvulsants
        Levetiracetam (Keppra)
        Carbamazepine (Tegretol)
        Gabapentin (Neurontin)
        Oxycabazepine (Trileptal)
        Topiramate (Topamax)
        Zonisamide (Zonegran)

    C. Benzodiazepines
        Clonazepam (Klonopin)
        Alprazolam (Xanax)
        Lorazepam (Ativan)

    D. Calcium channel inhibitors
        Verapamil (Calan)
        Nifedipine (Procardia)
        Nimodipine (Nimoptop)
        Isradipine (DynaCirc)
        Amlodipine (Norvasc)
        Nicardipine (Cardene)
        Nisoldipine (Sular)

II. Antidepressants

    A. Serotonin-specific reuptake inhibitors
        Citalopram (Celexa)
        Escitalopram (Lexapro)
        Fluoxetine (Prozac, Sarafem)
        Fluvoxamine (LuVox)
        Paraxetine (Paxil)
        Sertraline (Zoloft)

B. Tertiary amine tricyclic antidepressants
   Amitriptyline (Elavil, Endep)
   Clomipramine (Anafranil)
   Dexepin (Adapin, Sinequan)
   Imipramine (Tofranil)
   Trimipramine (Surmontil)

C. Secondary amine tricyclic antidepressants
   Desipramine (Norpramin)
   Nortriptyline (Pamelor, Aventyl)
   Portriptyline (Vivactil)

D. Tetracyclic antidepressants
   Amoxapine (Asendin)
   Maprotiline (Ludiomil)
   Mirtazapine (Remeron)

E. Monoamine oxidase inhibitors
   Phenelzine (Nardil)
   Tranylcypromine (Parnate)

F. Atypical antidepressants
   Bupropion (Wellbutrin and Wellbutrin SR)
   Duloxetine (Cymbalta)
   Nefazodone (Serzone)
   Trazadone (Desyrel)
   Venlafaxine (Effexor and Effexor XR)

III. Attention-deficit hyperactivity disorder (ADHD)

A. Psychostimulants
   Dextroamphetamine + Amphetamine (Adderall)
   Dextroamphetamine (Dexadrine)
   Methyphenidate (Concerta, Metadate, Methylin, Ritalin,
     Focalin)
   Pemoline (Cylert)

B. Atomexetine (Strattera)

C. Alpha Agonists
    Clonidine (Catapress)
    Guanfacine (Tenex)

D. Antidepressants
    Bupropin (Wellbutrin)
    Venlafaxine (Effexor)

E. Narcolepsy medication
    Modafinil (Provigil)

IV. Antipsychotics—Neuroleptics

A. High-potency antipsychotics
    Fluphenazine (Prolixin)
    Haloperidol (Haldol)
    Pimozide (Orap)
    Thiothixene (Navane)
    Trifluoperazine (Stelazine)

B. Midpotency antipsychotics
    Loxapine (Loxitane)
    Molindone (Moban)
    Perphenazine (Trilafon)

C. Low-potency antipsychotics
    Chlorpromazine (Thorazine)
    Mesoridazine (Serentil)
    Thioridazine (Mellaril)

D. Atypical antipsychotics
    Aripiprazole (Abilify)
    Clozapine (Clozaril)
    Risperidone (Risperdal)
    Olanzapine (Zyprexa, Zydus)
    Quetiapine (Seroquel)
    Ziprasidone (Geodon)

THE AUTHORS

Dr. Les Carter is the senior psychotherapist at the Minirth Clinic in Richardson, Texas, where he has maintained a practice since 1980, specializing in the treatment of emotional and relational disorders. He is the author of eighteen books, including *The Anger Trap, The Anger Workbook, The Worry Workbook, The Freedom from Depression Workbook,* and *People Pleasers.* He received his bachelor's degree from Baylor University and his master's and Ph.D. degrees from the University of North Texas.

A popular speaker, Carter leads seminars in cities across America. He can be reached at www.AngerExpert.com.

Dr. Frank Minirth is president of the Minirth Clinic in Richardson, Texas. He has authored or coauthored more than sixty books, including the bestsellers *Happiness Is a Choice, Love Is a Choice,* and *Love Hunger.* He holds degrees from Arkansas State University, Arkansas School of Medicine, Christian Bible College, and Dallas Theological Seminary, where he is an adjunct professor.

He serves as a consultant for the Minirth Christian Group at Green Oaks Behavioral Healthcare Services in Dallas and at the Minirth Christian Services at Millwood Hospital in Arlington, Texas. For more information, please call 888-646-4784 or go to www.minirthclinic.com.

The Anger Trap

*Free Yourself
from the Frustrations
That Sabotage Your Life*

Dr. Les Carter

Hardcover
ISBN: 0-7879-6879-X

"*The Anger Trap* is a masterfully written book, offering penetrating insights into the factors that can imprison individuals in unwanted patterns of frustration. With his well-developed insights and using case examples, Les Carter carefully explains how you can change your thinking, your communication, and your behavior as you release yourself from the ravages of anger gone bad."

—from the Foreword by Frank Minirth, M.D.

"Les Carter has assimilated his years of experience counseling people trapped by anger into a book that I believe will prove helpful to many readers. *The Anger Trap* offers fresh information and understanding that can lead to recovery and reconciliation." —Zig Ziglar, author and motivational speaker

"The best book on anger out there. Five stars!" —Dr. Tim Clinton, president, American Association of Christian Counselors

Dr. Les Carter—a nationally recognized expert on the topics of conflict resolution, emotions, and spirituality and coauthor of the best-selling *The Anger Workbook*—has written this practical book that strips away common myths and misconceptions to show viable ways to overcome unhealthy anger and improve relationships. With gentle spiritual wisdom and solid psychological research, Dr. Carter guides you to creating a better, happier life for yourself, your family, and your coworkers.

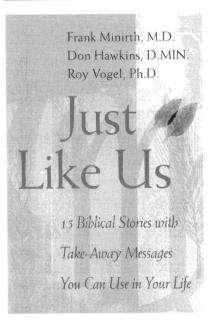

Frank Minirth, M.D.
Don Hawkins, D.MIN.
Roy Vogel, Ph.D.

Just
Like Us

15 Biblical Stories with

Take-Away Messages

You Can Use in Your Life

Just Like Us

15 Biblical Stories with
Take-Away Messages
You Can Use in Your Life

Frank Minirth, Ph.D., M.D.
Don Hawkins, D. Min.
Roy Vogel, Ph.D.

Hardcover
ISBN: 0-7879-6904-4

In *Just Like Us* a psychologist, psychia-
trist, and minister use their evaluations
of fifteen major biblical figures—including Moses, David, and Martha—
to explore how ordinary people fit into God's plan. This compelling book
helps to bring its readers to a greater understanding of these figures while recognizing that people of the Bible were just like us, with similar strengths, frail-
ties, and struggles. The authors emphasize take-home messages at each chapter's
end and include personal reflection questions.

Frank Minirth, Ph.D., M.D., is president of the Minirth Clinic in Richardson,
Texas, and has authored or coauthored approximately fifty books.

Don Hawkins, D. Min., is a veteran conference and seminar speaker who cur-
rently hosts the live call-in program "Life Perspectives" from Southeastern
Bible College in Birmingham.

Roy Vogel, Ph.D., is vice president/clinical director of the Christian Health
Care Center's Advent Counseling Centers.

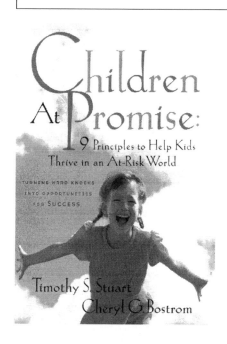

Children At Promise

9 Principles to Help Kids Thrive in an At-Risk World

Tim Stuart, Ed.D.
Cheryl Bostrom, M.A.

Hardcover
ISBN: 0-7879-6875-7

"Tim Stuart and Cheryl Bostrom offer a unique and practical perspective on how to have a godly, eternal impact on children. Their message is especially critical to those young people whose lives have been characterized by disappointment and rejection."
—Dr. Bill Bright, founder and president of Campus Crusade for Christ

"Every child is bound to bump into tough times and these experiences are sure to shape their character for good or ill. *Children At Promise* is an immensely practical and inspirational tool for helping kids rise above adversity—and succeed not only in spite of it, but because of it. This book is a winner!"
—Les Parrott, Ph.D., professor of clinical psychology, Seattle Pacific University; author, *Helping Your Struggling Teenager*

In today's complex world filled with violence, drugs, and confusing sexual messages, these and other threats to our young people have prompted educators, politicians, and government agencies to label our children as "at risk" of failure. Although intended to be a way of identifying those who need help, this label can cause us to taint our language and behaviors toward young people with hopelessness and defeat. But there is hope. *Children At Promise* maintains that all children can be viewed with positive expectancy and shows how we parents, grandparents, educators, and friends can help to fulfill our children's deep potential. In this inspirational and informative book, high school principal Tim Stuart, Ed.D. and former teacher-of-the-year Cheryl Bostrom, M.A., offer easy-to-understand, research-based evidence for the power of nurturing the promise in all children regardless of the risks they experience. Stuart and Bostrom's unique, revolutionary approach to child rearing emphasizes the true identity of all children and their caregivers, the importance of relationship, and the value of adversity. Solidly grounded in tested educational and psychological theory as well as with timeless biblical wisdom, *Children At Promise* provides parents and educators with the insights, motivation, and tools for raising successful children of P.R.O.M.I.S.E. character.

Printed in the United States
By Bookmasters